You Can Write a

Memoir

To Dad -
with love.
yes you
should!!
do it.
etc.
Sully,
Ned &
Grant

Susan Carol Hauser

D0823931

W

WRITER'S DIGEST BOOKS
Cincinnati, Ohio
www.writersdigest.com

You Can Write a Memoir. Copyright © 2001 by Susan Carol Hauser. Manufactured in the United States of America. All rights reserved. No part of this book may be reproduced in any form or by any electronic or mechanical means including information storage and retrieval systems without permission in writing from the publisher, except by a reviewer, who may quote brief passages in a review. Published by Writer's Digest Books, an imprint of F&W Publications, Inc., 1507 Dana Avenue, Cincinnati, Ohio 45207. (800) 289-0963. First edition.

Visit our Web site at www.writersdigest.com for information on more resources for writers.

To receive a free weekly e-mail newsletter delivering tips and updates about writing and about Writer's Digest products, send an e-mail with the message "Subscribe Newsletter" to newsletter-request@writersdigest.com, or register directly at our Web site at http://newsletters.fwpublications.com.

05 04 03 02 01   5 4 3 2 1

Library of Congress Cataloging-in-Publication Data

Hauser, Susan
  You can write a memoir / by Susan Carol Hauser
    p.   cm.
  Includes index.
  ISBN 0-89879-998-8 (alk. paper)
    1. Autobiography—Authorship. 2. Report writing. I. Title.

CT25 .H38   2001
808'.06692—dc21   00-054542
                                                                 CIP

Edited by Jack Heffron and Donya Dickerson
Designed by Angela Wilcox
Cover designed by Lisa Buchanan
Cover photography by © TSM/John Henley, 1997
Production coordinated by Mark Griffin

The author thanks Loonfeather Press for permission to use "To See the Other Side" and "Lessons" from *Meant to Be Read Out Loud*; "Lighting the Way" from *Which Way to Look*; and "The Animals at Home" from *What the Animals Know*.

Student essays reprinted with permission of authors.

In memory of my parents,
Ada Louise Fields Hauser
and Howard John Hauser,
the wellspring of my stories.

About the Author

Susan Carol Hauser's books include *Full Moon: Reflections on Turning Fifty* and *Sugartime: The Hidden Pleasures of Making Maple Syrup*. She teaches writing at Bemidji State University in Minnesota and is a commentator on National Public Radio. Excerpts from her books may be viewed at www.intraart.com. She lives in northern Minnesota.

Books by Susan Carol Hauser

Natural History

Outwitting Ticks: The Prevention and Treatment of Lyme Disease and Other Ailments Caused by Ticks, Scorpions, Spiders and Mites

Wild Rice Cooking: History, Natural History, Harvesting and Lore, With Recipes

Sugartime: The Hidden Pleasures of Making Maple Syrup

Nature's Revenge: The Secrets of Poison Ivy, Poison Oak and Poison Sumac and Their Remedies

Nonfiction

Full Moon: Reflections on Turning Fifty

Girl to Woman: A Gathering of Images

Which Way to Look

Meant to Be Read Out Loud

What the Animals Know

Poetry

Redpoll on a Broken Branch

Contents

CHAPTER ONE

Writing a Memoir

We all have memories. They are the well from which we draw stories. And most of us have a desire to tell and hear stories, even short ones, as witnessed by the energetic conversation around our dinner tables and by standard questions that open many of our social conversations: "What are you up to?" "What did you do today?" "What's going on?" Some of us have the desire to write those stories, to use them to preserve our personal or family histories, and to write ourselves into the present and even the future.

When we are children, stories come to us easily: We tell them for the sake of the telling, without an awareness of what they tell about us, what they might mean to others or what their larger meanings may be about the human experience. We are not bothered by notions of fact or truth, for the truth is in the telling. As adults, however, the simple desire to tell our stories becomes fraught with the necessity of making choices. Who will tell the story? The child who experienced it? The mother who watched? The father who remembers? The adult child who wants to capture the past?

The common denominator in each of these perspectives is memory, which is the foundation of the memoir. The words *memoir* and *memory* come to us from the middle English/Anglo-French word *memorie*, and from the Latin *memoria*, derived from *memor*, which means "mindful." If the etymology of *memoir* is traced back far enough, as it is in *The American Heritage Dictionary of the English Language,* Third Edition, we also find a link to the Old Norse *Mimir,* "a giant who guards the well of wisdom." Related words that share the history of *memoir* include *remember, commemorate, memorable, memento* and *memorandum.* Surprisingly, the word *mourn* also shares its derivations and means "to remember sorrowfully" (*American Heritage*).

Memory is common to other types of personal writing, among them the daybook, diary, journal and autobiography. Yet each of these, including the memoir, has distinct qualities.

The daybook is a record of daily transactions. Writers sometimes use one to keep notes for story ideas and to briefly record experiences, thoughts or emotions that intrigue them. The daybook is usually kept in the form of a list, rather than in paragraphs or stories.

Some dictionaries consider the terms *daybook* and *diary* synonymous, being two names for one thing, and they do derive from the same word root, *dei,* meaning "shine," which gives us our words for day and deity. But for me, the diary goes one step beyond the listing of daily transactions: It develops events, thoughts and emotions of the day into longer passages—paragraphs and sometimes pages. In the diary, we conjecture about the meaning of the events of the day, and contemplate and meditate on their value in our lives; in the daybook we merely record occurrences.

The word *journal* also comes to us from the root *dei* and the word *shine,* by way of the word *diurnal,* which means "daily," or "a twenty-four hour period." Most dictionaries list it as a synonym for diary, but again I have a different sense of it. Writers today, I think, use a journal as a place to write about their experiences, thoughts and emotions without much concern for the day of occurrence.

The daybook, diary and journal have something in common beyond their etymologies: They are all written with the self as audience. Although others may, of course, read them, the writer is generally speaking internally, recording or working out experience for the sake of it or for self-memory. Two other forms of writing that are predicated on personal memory differ from this in a significant way: the autobiography and the memoir are written instead with an audience in mind.

The autobiography on the surface is concerned with the chronology, the timeline, of a life. It generally starts at a given date and progresses through the years to another date. But, as we all know, there is more to life than dates, and the sound autobiography includes consideration of family, society and culture, even politics and history—the soup we swim in and that gives our lives meaning.

The memoir—the subject of this book—while sharing with autobiography the notion of audience, differs from it in at least one significant way: It is not necessarily concerned with the chronology of things nor does it have to move from date to date. Rather, it might be concerned with themes that recur within a chronology, such as a memoir about birthdays throughout one person's life. Or it might be concerned with a place, or another person, or any subject chosen by the writer. Further, the subject of a memoir might be confined to a single day in the writer's life, or it might draw from days plucked from the string of the entire life.

While all five of these genres—daybook, diary, journal, autobiography and memoir—are pulled from the well of personal experience, of memory, the distinction of audience applied to autobiography and memoir lift them into writing on a different plane than the others. The mere recording of events, mere recollection, and even contemplation and meditation are usually not enough in themselves to warrant an audience. Writers who would speak to others, who would be heard by others, will want to make the transition from "this is my story" to "this is the story of a human life, and it is therefore also your story."

The distinction is sometimes subtle and sometimes hard to achieve. Other times it might be clear and achieved spontaneously. Elevating your personal story to a more universal level is a frequent topic in the coming chapters, in which I will guide you through the challenging, exciting, frightening and ultimately satisfying experience of writing a memoir.

Experiments

1. The Desire to Write. Although the desire to write a memoir might be enough in itself to inspire you to sit down and start writing, thinking about why you want to write a memoir can be helpful. Your answers might help form your writing and give it direction. Try composing a few sentences or paragraphs about your desire to write a memoir. Do you remember when you first thought of it? Did a certain event or object or memory trigger the desire? Do you have an end goal for your writing, such as passing on family history? Or is the writing itself your end goal, to be read the way we listen to music, just for the sake of it?

2. Writing for Posterity: Remembering So We Don't Forget. Although it may be true that we have some genetic history stored in the biologic library of our bodies, unless we preserve the stories of our personal lives, they will almost certainly be lost to the relentless passage of time.

Some of the stories are successfully perpetuated through oral tradition, through their telling and retelling at holiday dinners, and at reunions of family and friends. These stories take on the sheen of well-polished stones and carry within them the warmth of generations.

A similar warmth may be inspired through the writing and reading of personal histories, including the history of the family, nonfamilial groups such as neighborhoods, or circles of friends or individuals who shine in some way in their own right.

If you are writing to preserve a memory, make a list, or some notes, or write a page or two about what you want to preserve. If you can, say why—although sometimes knowing you want to create the record is enough.

3. Writing for the Sake of Writing. Often, experienced writers have a yen to work on a project without knowing why or where the project will end up. They are not bothered by this uncertainty because they understand that writing is not the mere reporting of facts-in-evidence. They know that it is a process of imagination and creation, and that the story will unfold not from some predetermined plot but from the telling of the story.

Perhaps there are subjects you want to write about but don't know why? Maybe they are mere images, pictures in the mind or portions of memories. Without concern for purpose or end goals, make a list of some things that occur to you to write about. Expand your list by adding descriptions, comments or questions to each of the subjects.

CHAPTER TWO

Writing About Childhood, Writing From Mementos

During the process of conjuring this book, I sought a way to organize the chapters. I turned to chronology, that natural and ever present form of order that permeates our lives. And so this chapter is on writing about childhood, followed by chapters on adolescence and adulthood.

Writing about childhood can be difficult because of its distance from us in time. But in some ways, it is the easiest time of our lives to write about. This is due in part to the same reason that it is difficult—because of its distance from us in time—but also because our childhood lives are, for the most part, blissfully unencumbered by thought and perspective. Our lives as children generally take place in the moment and are replete with memory securely tied to our senses: What we remember from childhood frequently comes to us through experiences of taste, touch, sight, sound and smell.

Taste, touch, sight, sound, smell. The five senses. A treasure trove of memory. If I say to you, "What year did you go to kindergarten?" you probably have to do some math. "Let's see, I would have been five years old, and I was born in 19xx, therefore. . . ." And while you are doing the calculations, some other part of your brain is starting to call up from its archives pictures of your kindergarten experience. You might say, "Well, we lived in Richfield at the time. I remember that I had to take a bus all by myself." And quickly you lose interest in the year, and you are redrawing the bus, the street, the yard, the house, your mother standing with you on the curb.

Such thoughts provide an order for memory that is different from the order provided by chronology. It is the order of the senses, of shapes, colors, tastes, textures and scents. In writing, we call it imagery, because it conjures for us an image, a picture. We *imagine* the scene: "I remember that the bus was orange and that it seemed to come straight at us, its wheels kicking up dust from the dirt road, and its engine drowning out all sound, and even thought."

In the end, imagery, as with imagination, is mysterious to us. I certainly don't understand how it carries all that it does, for the image almost always conveys more than it presents on the surface. The child waiting for the school bus makes me think of more than a child at a moment in time. It allows me also to think of the poignant feelings of childhood, of feeling small compared to a bus in motion; of feeling alone, even though mother is standing next to me; of anticipation mixed with fear. Even the bus represents something to me, perhaps the unwieldy, uncontrollable, unknown future. The bus stops for me, and I get on and ride off into the rest of my life.

Imagery and Details

Wait a minute, you might want to say to me. All I want to do is write about my childhood. I want to remember it, and I want my children and grandchildren to know about it. What does imagery have to do with that? Can't I just say, "I lived here at this time, and the house was painted white, and there were three pine trees in the yard, and we moved away when I was thirteen"?

Yes, you can say that, and recording memory in that way is a good way to get started on a writing project. But when most of us write, we want to convey more than the details of our lives. We want to convey the meaning of our lives and the lives of those around us.

In a way, this type of writing is not so difficult to do. Even the sparse description of my childhood home is built on sensory detail: a house, a white house, trees, pine trees. These are all things I can see in my mind's eye, and they begin to let me see what it was like for that writer to live in their childhood.

It is, in fact, difficult to write without using imagery and sensory detail. About the only place we accomplish it is in legal documents, which may be why they are so hard to read. There are no images for us to hang the details on, no convenient way for our brains to organize the information. We have only abstractions and concepts, such as ownership and responsibility.

Abstractions, or ideas, are in a way the flip side of imagery. The two are often paired as a dichotomy. Ideas are abstract; imagery is concrete: abstract vs. concrete. Something that is concrete is known through the senses. Something that is abstract is known only in the mind. Love is abstract; a hug is concrete. Fear is abstract; a person teetering on the edge of a cliff is concrete.

We use this dichotomy all the time. I might say to you, "I want to travel," which is abstract, an idea. Then I might say, "I want to travel to Kenya to see the animals at home," which is concrete, a visualization of the abstract desire. Or I might say to you, "My knees were shaking and my palms were wet with sweat,"—a concrete, imagistic description. And you might think to yourself, "Ah, she was afraid."

As we do in our thinking, in our conversations and even in our memories, we use both abstract and concrete writing to tell our stories. When you tell the story of your childhood, it can help to think sometimes about both the abstract and the concrete. Sometimes the concrete can be used to illustrate an idea; sometimes an idea can emerge from a concrete image.

You might say, "Concrete, abstract, who cares? I just want to write about my childhood."

Hmmm—that's a good abstract statement. What made you think of it? Do you have memories of a place, a person, a feeling, an event? Make a list of them. Opposite the concrete items, write a couple of abstract words that go with the images. For example, after *red wagon* you might write *freedom, responsibility* or *play*. Grandmother's four-poster bed might elicit feelings of warmth and security. Do the opposite for abstract terms. *Christmas*, which is an idea, might be paired with *Christmas tree, Christmas cookies, the crèche, presents to open. Fear* might be paired with *swimming for the first time.*

This list can provide some of the lumber (concrete/image) you will use to build your childhood memoir (abstract/idea). And it can help you see ways to organize your memoir that aren't chronological. You might decide to write a chapter on places, one on people, one on major life events. Or you might see in your list ways to organize your memoir chronologically, but with chapter breaks determined not by the chronological year, but according to places you lived, your birth date, summers or school years.

Leaps of Faith

The hardest part about writing for most of us is not coming up with ideas about what we want to write, or in the case of the memoir, remembering the past. The hardest part is starting to write. The blank page is a frightening landscape. It has no signposts, no horizon. It does not tell us where we were, where we are or where we are going. All of that must come from our hearts and must pass through our minds onto the page. Every time I sit down to a new writing project, with a new blank file open on my computer screen, I say, sometimes out loud, "What ever made me think I wanted to do this?"

I think the "leap of faith" recommended by the philosopher Søren Kierkegaard—belief in God without proof of God's existence—applies well to writing. Once you have had an urge to write, try to let the urge itself carry you through those first writing sessions, where you are wandering in the wilderness of your memory, looking for a rock to sit on, from which you can observe and then write about your past.

Your landscape, of course, might be riddled with rocks to sit on, and then you get to make a second leap of faith. You get to place your trust in an image. If you are sitting down to write and you have in front of you a list of five or six childhood objects or moments, almost certainly one of them will call you back to it over and over. It won't seem like much of an image. Maybe it is only your dad's hammer or your mother's iron. Maybe it is the doll's dress Aunt Maude made for you. Because thought, creativity and emotion are mysterious to us, and because they occur in our minds and hearts at depths we do not have easy access to, you might not know immediately what possibilities the images hold. But some part of you knows and tells you that by calling you back to the image again and again.

If none of the images flashes at you above the others, write a few sentences or paragraphs about each one. Describe in exquisite, even torturous, detail what you see. "Auntie's tea cup has a crack on the side away from the handle. An ivy vine twines all the way around the bowl of the cup and is repeated on the saucer." Then try using the images to describe something about the people who use the objects: "An ivy vine twines all the way around the bowl of the cup and is repeated on the saucer, the way the color of my mother's eyes is repeated in her sister's eyes."

The story is in the details. And not just any details, but in the details that occur to you. You will learn, through practice, to recognize details that are ripe with possibility, and you can become skilled at letting the details tell your story for you. "The school bus, orange and monstrous, came toward me the way life does when you are small, and when it stopped for me, I gave up my mother's hand and climbed aboard, sat on the edge of my seat and let myself be carried away.''

Using Comparisons

Comparison, such as comparing life to a school bus, or a cup and saucer to my mother and auntie, is a common literary device. We use it in our everyday stories: ''I'm as limp as a dishrag''; ''I felt like a kid again.'' It is the stuff of poetry: ''My love is like a red, red rose'' (Robert Burns). It is the basis of song lyrics, especially country-western lyrics: ''She was a T-bone talkin' woman but she had a hot-dog heart.'' And it can be the device that turns a ho-hum life story into a heartfelt, even passionate memoir.

There are many terms for literary comparison. An analogy is a comparison. A simile is an analogy that states the comparison says how the one thing is similar to the other: ''Love is like rain.'' A metaphor removes the statement of comparison: ''Love is rain.'' A symbol is a comparison but goes one step further than simple analogy. A symbol claims that the subject and the comparison are more than similar; one *is* the other. For example, the Stars and Stripes are a symbol for the United States of America. But the flag is not compared to the U.S.; rather, it substitutes for it. If we burn the flag, some might say, we burn the country. If I break my auntie's tea cup, I might also be saying that I am breaking with the past or breaking with Auntie. The orange school bus carries me not only to school, but away from my mother.

Sometimes we refer to such comparisons as figures

of speech or as figurative language. This echoes the use of the word *image*, because a figure is a shape and is therefore concrete.

Our richest writing often uses language that is both figurative and literal. *Literal* means "actual" and comes from the same word root as do *literary* and *literature*, from the Latin *littera*, "letter." Literally, the bus carried me to school; figuratively, it carried me away from mother and into the rest of my life.

It is not necessary to know these terms and their definitions in order to write a memoir, but it can help to recognize the usefulness and power of comparison. The device can help our readers understand in a meaningful way experiences that they have not had. Because I have broken objects and because I have broken from some parts of my own past, when the writer links these two things for me, I can more easily know the experience being described.

Finding the Meaning

Comparison can add another dimension to our writing: It can allow us to articulate the value or meaning behind an experience, and put it in perspective. If I write only, "I stood at the bus stop with my mother and then got on the bus and went to school," I have given a snapshot of what happened. But events and moments themselves have limited value as stories. Stories almost always tell us something in addition to their plot line, to the sequence of events. They tell us why the event is important. I remember getting on the bus not because I got on the bus for the first time but because by getting on the bus I was also stepping into my future, which was unknown to me. Of course I could not have said that at the time, but some part of me remembers, and the memory is held in my mind and heart in the concrete image of that bus.

Images rarely fail us. Each one, like a picture, is worth a thousand words.

Images and even some of the ideas from our childhood may be held in the mind of the child that still resides, in some ways, within us. But it is the adult in us who calls forth the images and ideas, and puts them on that blank sheet of paper. Once again, we are faced with creative choices: Who gets to do the talking here? The child? The adult child? The adult? Somebody's wife, husband, mother or father?

The perspective we choose to write from is called the voice of the writer. Although I describe the school bus the way I saw it as a child, I write the child's description with my adult voice. It is one of the pleasures of writing a memoir: We get to recall our experiences in any way we want and to frame them any way we want. I could frame the story of the school bus with notions of fear, or notions of excitement, or notions of abandonment. Which to choose? I want to tell the truth. But the truth is, when I write, I *create* truth. If I step into the open arms of the bus, I am implying a positive experience. If I step into the open maw of the bus and stare down the aisle at the rows of seats gleaming in the early sun like the teeth of a whale, I am implying a negative experience. To create an accurate truth, I must try different ways to present the image and choose the version that does the job at hand, which is not only to tell my story, but to tell it so it can be felt as well as heard by my readers.

Discovering the Truth

Memoirists generally assume that someone else will read their stories (or else they would write diaries or journals), and they hope their readers will discover within the stories truths not only about the characters in the memoir but about themselves as readers. But we forget sometimes that we, as writers, are also an audience for our own writing. One of the hardest things to do as a writer is to allow yourself to discover, through your writing, truths about yourself and your experiences. When I first wrote the scenario about the orange school bus, I expected it to be useful to talk about the vulnerability of children, about how small we are, and how big and orange life is. But each time I came back to the example, I found myself expanding the memory. As I did, my mother started to come into focus, and I realized that she also has a story to tell about that moment. As I think about it now, I realize that she might have felt more alone than I did, and it evokes a sadness in me. As children we feel so much but are able to feel so little for others. This is a realization I am not particularly happy about, but still I feel good that I can let it in.

Such sudden realizations add a layer to childhood memoirs that bring them forward out of the past and into the present. Telling the story of my discovery along with the story remembered can deepen the value of the memoir for both the reader and the writer. And the realization can lead to another story. Now when I think about telling the story of the school bus, I think I might write it twice: once from my perspective and once from my mother's. I can intertwine the stories, or I can tell them separately.

There is yet another story that might emerge: The mother and the child might take on lives of their own and bring to me a story that did not happen to me, but is one that wants to be told. Such stories are called fiction. If this happens to you, you might feel blessed or cursed. "But I want to tell *my* story," you might say. And you will, even if you tell a story that never was true, except in the writing.

Experiments

1. Writing From Mementos: Places, Objects, Photographs. Often our memories are locked into objects that we carry with us from place to place in our lives. I have my mother's sewing scissors, my father's enamel coffeepot and my grandparents' cuckoo clock. I don't use any of them—the scissors are faulty, I don't make coffee on the stove and the clock refuses to keep time. Still, it gives me pleasure to have them handy.

I enjoy a similar pleasure when I visit places that are special to me—the park where the family picnicked, the house we lived in for my first thirteen years—and when I look at photographs from my past. Sometimes a sound will also trigger a memory. As an adult, I lived for a while in a neighborhood that had an ice-cream truck. I could hear its tinny song coming from a half-block away, before I could see the truck. I have no surface memory of an ice-cream truck in my childhood, but every time I heard that tune, I wept spontaneously. Similarly, smells bring forth a swelling of remembrance, especially cooking odors like the sweet smells of cakes and cookies.

All of these memories have a common denominator: They are linked to the five senses—taste, touch, sight, sound and scent. For reasons no one understands very well, the senses are one of the memory trunks of the brain. And for reasons also mysterious, when we tell the story of the object, place, sound or smell that we remember, we also tell our own story.

Look around for objects from your past. Hold them; put them up where you can look at them. Drive through the old neighborhood. Talk with family and friends about your mutual past. After a few days, choose one topic to make notes about. First, make notes about your subject, but do not start to write your story yet. Only describe the subject in intricate detail.

Next, make notes about the role the subject played in your life. If you are looking at a picture of your childhood home, for example, describe what you literally see in the picture: the size, shape and location of the house.

Now you might be ready to write your story. Read over your notes again, then set them aside. They were useful to call forward details about your subject. Now that those details are fresh in your memory, let them play out in the story as they occur to you while you write, referring to your notes only occasionally for a detail or phrase you were pleased with.

You can start your story any way that occurs to you. You might say, "I remember . . ." or "I have had the photograph since we moved away from 1201 West Seventy-third Street." As you tell the story, look for analogies that might reveal to you and your reader more than the story of the object, look for the figurative meaning in the object. "The skin of the basketball has thinned and is deflated, as I sometimes feel compared to the boy who made the winning shot in the high school tournament."

A writing such as this might help you start writing your memoir, or it can be one of many pieces, or vignettes, that you gather together into a memoir.

2. *Writing From a Notion.* Not all of our memories are triggered by reconnection with their sensory value of taste, touch, sight, sound or smell. Sometimes an experience or idea will trigger a memory for us, though the memory itself is usually grounded in sensory images. When we write from notions, ideas and memories that just "come to mind," we can make them descriptive through the use of sensory details. And it can be easier to discover the value of such memories, because often the value comes to us first. "I remember the first time I rode my bike." As with the previous exercise on writing from mementos, start by making notes about memories you hold in your mind (rather than in a picture or an object). Then set the notes aside while you write their stories.

Here are some ideas that might harbor memories for you. You can probably think of others.

- The first time you read a book on your own.
- The first time you got lost.
- Other "firsts," including your first memory.
- The time you traveled alone.
- The family vacation that went awry.
- The family vacation that did not go awry.
- People who made a difference to you in your childhood, including parents, siblings, other relatives, even strangers.
- A place that is now gone, removed by development or kept from you by geographical distance. (It might also be kept from you figuratively—by your distance from it in time.)

3. Letting Fiction Take Over. Whenever we write, we usually mix truth with fiction. Intuitively, we exaggerate in order to relay not just the facts of an event or a time, but the feeling of it. Sometimes this is called poetic license—the freedom of the writer to tell the story as it needs to be told.

In order to loosen up your writing, to become more comfortable with poetic license, you can try writing little stories in which your real-life characters or places become fictional ones. Let things happen that did not happen.

You might be surprised at how easy this is to do. Our minds seem to love telling stories. "There was a girl standing at the bus stop with her mother. She was five years old and was going off to school for the first time. What her mother did not know was . . ."

The point of this experiment is not to write fiction but to tap your innate ability to imagine, to fill in the blanks in your memory. The only risk is that the story you make up might demand to be written instead of your memoir. If that happens, let it happen. You can always write your memoir at the same time or later. Someday one of the stories you tell might be about the day you discovered you were a fiction writer.

4. Other Experiments. Look ahead to the experiments for chapter three, writing about the teenage years, and chapter four, writing about adult life. The techniques used there also work for writing about childhood.

CHAPTER THREE

Writing About Adolescence and Other Life Changes

We are between experiences many times in our lives but probably never as often as we are during our teen-age years. Here's a between story of mine.

To See the Other Side

One of my strongest teenage memories comes from a family springtime vacation in Florida. It was my first visit to the ocean. I stayed close to shore when we went swimming and watched with disbelief as my father stroked out beyond the breakers and floated like a piece of driftwood in the calm water that stretched clear out to the horizon and beyond.

I think it was not the depth of the water that fright-ened me so much as its distance. I found it hard to believe that you could not see the other side. In my determination to bring infinity under control, I aban-doned the facts of the curvature of the Earth and the sheer distance between the continents and decided that I would look hard enough, and long enough, and I would see France.

For several days I sat on the beach of the Atlantic Ocean and stared east. I let my eyes adjust, then re-adjust, to the light and to the motion of the waves. Sometimes I squinted and peered. Other times I stared, keeping my eyes open even though they watered, and the brightness entered them like sand. I was determined to be honest about this. Mist would not be misconstrued as land. Boats on the horizon would be simply boats, not land or buildings. When my brothers and sisters asked what I was doing, I told them, "trying to see the other side." They did not believe me but left me alone.

I wrote this memory quite a few years ago. It is perhaps a pure example of a young adult story. I was old enough, experienced enough, to think about the other side, and young enough, innocent enough, not to be hampered by logic. I was on the way to coming-of-age, but clearly I was not there yet.

Coming-of-age is a literary term used to describe the passage from childhood to adulthood, from a state of innocence to a state of experience. Most writing about the teenage years is about coming-of-age, for that is the point of those years. We slip free of the protection and constraints of childhood and step into the vulnerability and freedom of adulthood, and we know it.

This interpretation, my interpretation, might seem backward to some: Is it not true that in childhood we are vulnerable but free, and in adulthood we have power but are constrained? It is an ancient conundrum, told best perhaps in the story of the Garden of Eden. Adam and Eve lived a riddle-free life until they acquired knowledge. Having gained knowledge, they lost their innocence. They were thus both blessed and cursed.

This story is played out again in the passage of every one of us from child to adult. For most of us, it is a passage full of both blessings and curses. We fear the loss of our innocence as much as we crave knowledge of our experience.

For me, writings about this stage of life fall into a trilogy of neat phases. The first phase includes stories about the cusp between innocence and experience, the period of time just before the crossing-over. This is the phase I assign to the excerpt from my story about trying to see the other side of the ocean. The second phase includes stories about the crossing-over itself, the coming-of-age stories. Stories in the third phase reflect back on the crossing.

I am pleased about the tidiness of these distinctions, because so little is neat about those years. Still, the distinctions are arbitrary and are not exclusive. Many memoirs about how teen years pass use all three phases. For example, my story about the ocean continues this way:

I did not see the ocean again for many years, and I think I was glad to let go of the knowledge that there are things I cannot do no matter how hard I try. Back at home, the same year as the trip to the Atlantic, I entered the water of summer as I always had. I swam in it, floated on it and cut through it with the knife of a boat.

That summer I learned that water is also something to walk around. Nearly every night a girlfriend and I walked the few blocks from our houses down to the lake, and then set ourselves onto the path around it.

Out on the water, sailboats and waves came together like lovers. Along the shore, children darted, sowing sand in the small sea of the lake. And at any time we could look up and see the tree on the other side where we had started. We knew where we came from, and we knew where we were going.

Though I did not think about it at the time, it must have been a comfort to be, for a few minutes, on a journey that had a certain end. It is a pleasure I have not given up. I still like to go around something when I walk. If there is no lake, I walk around a block. If there is no block, I walk around a field. Sometimes, when I am in the country, I am forced to walk a ways down the road and then turn around abruptly and go back. It is an unnatural act, and besides, nothing is as right to walk around as water.

I have been back to the ocean many times as a grown-up, and it still frightens me. On one visit, with my brother and his family, my brother took me by the hand, led me into the water and taught me how to snorkel. We floated face down, our backs bobbling in the sun, the black pipes of the snorkeling tubes hooked into the air. The water was surprisingly clear, and I began to follow small fishes down a path of bright corals. At one point I glanced ahead. The depth and breadth of the ocean opened in front of me. There were no roads, there was no end. I could not see the other side.

I flew up out of the water and found myself standing just chest deep. Behind me, on the shore, the rest of the family lazed in the sun, unaware of the danger I perceived. I joined them, and we walked up the beach a ways and then back. I kept one eye on the horizon, though. Maybe now, being older, if I looked hard enough and long enough, I could see where I started from.

In this conclusion to my story, I come of age: I understand the vulnerabilities and limitations of the adult, and I accept them. I also reflect on the experience: I recognize that I no longer try to see the other side but do hold out the hope of seeing to the early side of my own life. The story thus moves through all three phases: the time prior to coming-of-age, the coming-of-age and the reflection on coming-of-age.

Not that I thought about any of that when I was doing the writing. I wanted to write something about that memory, to tell the story of it, and I did, with as much detail as I could conjure. I had done enough writing by then to trust the images that came to me, so when I also thought to write about walking around the lake and snorkeling, I did, as part of the same story. It is only now, talking about the story, that I see the other side of it. I see that it is not only my story; it is a story about coming-of-age.

Coming-of-Age

In the tidy world of the story, coming-of-age is something that happens once: A series of events or a single event leads us to the moment when we cross over into adulthood. In real life, I suspect that it is rare to move from childhood to adulthood in one step. Rather, through the teenage years we take many small steps across the wide band that separates the extremes of our lives.

As with my story about the ocean, the moment of crossing is often spontaneous. We do not predict it or set it up. It just happens, and it happens because we have matured in body and mind to a point where it can happen. Had I sat on the same shore as a five-year-old or snorkeled as a ten-year-old, it is not likely that my ocean story would have the same action or ending as it did for me as a teenager.

Because this maturation is so important to us, most societies, if not all, hold formal activities that signal its onset. The Christian church welcomes children into the fold as adults in its confirmation ceremony, as does Judaism in its bar mitzvah ceremony. High school graduation signifies a passage from dependency to responsibility. These ceremonies are sometimes called rites of passage because they are rituals that mark passage from childhood to adulthood.

Not all rites of passage, however, are formalized within institutions such as churches and schools. Sometimes they are rituals of a family or a culture. Participation in a championship sporting event, attendance at a birth or at the funeral of a parent or grandparent might constitute a rite of passage.

Sometimes a rite of passage is marked by the giving of a gift. For example, an older person might pass along to a younger person a gift that symbolizes maturity; an heirloom ring or watch might be given as a graduation present. In the American Indian culture, a spoon used for making maple sugar, usually carved with decorations, traditionally is passed on from woman to woman within a family. In our contemporary culture, a parent might hand over to a teenager the keys to the family car.

It is perhaps inevitable that coming-of-age stories are bittersweet. As children we are, after all, betrayed. Life is not what we thought it was, and our parents conspired to keep us in the dark about the darkness we would come to know. Never mind that we could not know it early on. We are still betrayed, not only by our parents but by life.

Across the turn of the nineteenth century, from about 1784 to 1805, the British poet William Blake wrote *Songs of Innocence and of Experience Shewing the Two Contrary States of the Human Soul.* The most well known of these poems are "The Lamb," a song of innocence, and "The Tyger," a song of experience.

The Lamb

LITTLE Lamb, who made thee?
Dost thou know who made thee?
Gave thee life, & bid thee feed
By the stream & o'er the mead;
Gave thee clothing of delight,
Softest clothing, wooly, bright;
Gave thee such a tender voice,
Making all the vales rejoice?
Little Lamb, who made thee?
Dost though know who made thee?
Little Lamb, I'll tell thee,

Little Lamb, I'll tell thee:
He is called by thy name,
For he calls himself a Lamb.
He is meek, & he is mild;
He became a little child.
I a child, & thou a lamb,
We are called by his name.
Little Lamb, God bless thee!
Little Lamb, God bless thee!

The Tyger

TYGER! Tyger! burning bright
In the forests of the night,
What immortal hand or eye
Could frame they fearful symmetry?
In what distant deeps or skies
Burnt the fire of thine eyes?
On what wings dare he aspire?
What the hand dare seize the fire?
And what shoulder, & what art,
Could twist the sinews of thy heart?
And when thy heart began to beat,
What dread hand? & what dread feet?
What the hammer? what the chain?
In what furnace was thy brain?
What the anvil? what dread grasp
Dare its deadly terrors clasp?
When the stars threw down their spears,
And water'd heaven with their tears,
Did he smile his work to see?
Did he who made the Lamb make thee?

Tyger! Tyger! burning bright
In the forests of the night,
What immortal hand or eye,
Dare frame they fearful symmetry?

When I look at these poems side by side, I am taken with how well they exemplify for me the two states of the human condition. "The Lamb" is simple in its presentation, lulling in its rhythms and in its certainty. "The Tyger" burns with questions.

Questions, and the struggle to answer them, are perhaps the foundation of our passage from innocence to experience. They are the horse we ride from the darkness into light or light into darkness, depending on our view of it. They are not the questions of the child: Why is the sky blue? How do they get the chicken inside the egg? They are questions about meaning, about value, about possibility and responsibility, about origins and endings.

It is purported that in 1946 as she lay on her deathbed, the American poet Gertrude Stein was asked, "What are the answers?" She allegedly replied, "No, no, what are the questions?" William Blake knew some of them. Each of us, having come of age, as did Adam and Eve, probably knows the questions of our own lives.

Body and Soul

The duality of innocence and experience is echoed in the duality of the body and the mind. As teenagers, we come of age physically as well as spiritually. Crossing through puberty can be graceful and joyous, but more often, at least in American culture, it is like crossing through a minefield: We don't know where the bombs are buried.

Sometimes, writing about those days brings them into focus and places them in the larger context not only of our individual lives, but of our lives as humans. We can recognize that in some ways we are merely passengers in our bodies, and that, like a train, they go where the track goes, and we are along for the ride. Sometimes we can also see how decisions we made and actions we took influenced our destination.

As when you write about other aspects of your teenage years, asking questions is a way to start writing about puberty. When did you become aware of changes in your body? Did your family have rituals that acknowledged the changes? Did you talk to your parents about it, your siblings or friends?

As you answer your questions, watch for images that might help you tell your story. Perhaps you had a favorite shirt that no longer fit you as your body filled out and grew upward. When you set aside the shirt, what else did you set aside? When you took on a new shirt, what did you take on with it?

Writing During the Teen Years

You do not have to wait until you are past your teenage years to write about them: You can do that while you are still in the thick of the experience. The writing may even help you choose a path for moving forward. You can keep a diary, and record events and thoughts as though you are a journalist. What happened today or yesterday? Who did you see? What foods did you eat? Did you go to a movie or read a book? These mundane details make up the larger picture of your life. After you have recorded them, try commenting on them. What do they say about your likes and dislikes, about the choices you make?

Just as adults might write about their adolescence to understand their adulthood, teenagers can sometimes understand their adolescence by writing about their childhood. Do you have a favorite story about growing up? Do you hold close to you a childhood fear that still has some power over you? These, along with the experiences of the moment, are proper subjects for a teenage memoir. They can sometimes illuminate for both the writer and the reader the experience of being in transit between childhood and adulthood. For additional approaches to writing about that passage, consider the techniques discussed in this and in other chapters.

Looking Back on Adolescence

Unlike childhood, where objects and places often trigger memories, teenage memories seem more often to start with events: a football game, a dance, a camping trip, a birth or death in the family. Because teen years are also full of questions, you might start writing about them by asking questions of yourself. The questions might be specific or broad. "What happened on my thirteenth birthday?" "Can I recall an event or a string of events that led to my coming-of-age?" "What did it mean to me when Grandma died?" Through this process, you can probably identify several events that led spontaneously to your coming-of-age.

In spite of Gertrude Stein's question, try answering your questions. Make lists of concrete details about the events—things that involve the five senses. Was it night, or day? What clothes were you wearing? What did your friends look like? What food was served? If you have a memento from that time, take it out and look at it. Maybe its shape or feel will give you some images to work with: the leather of a football, the broken strings on a tennis racket, your grandmother's sewing kit, the pen from your grandfather's desk, a stone from the beach where you had your first kiss.

Next, choose one of the events to write about. One of them probably draws you back to it, even though you might not remember a lot of detail or have any idea about its significance. Don't let that stop you. The significance will likely emerge in the writing.

Experiments

1. Thinking About Coming-of-Age. Coming-of-age is a common theme in movies, television shows, song lyrics and books. As you watch and listen, make note of coming-of-age stories. This exercise might help you think about such stories of your own.

2. Writing About Your Writing. When you have finished a story about your teen years, look at it in terms of the trilogy I described in this chapter: Does the story take place before your coming-of-age? During? After?

All three? Write some reflections on what the story means for you.

3. *Writing About Family Rites of Passage.* Another question: Is there a rite of passage that your family recognizes as a crossing-over from childhood to adulthood? Perhaps it is not talked about that way, it is just exercised and experienced. The passing over of the keys to the family car might be an example. And there may be more than one such rite in your family or different ones for men and women. Using the technique described in the first experiment, write about your teenage rites of passage.

4. *Writing About Your Personal Coming-of-Age.* Some of us have a singular moment in our past when we seemingly leapt in one jump from childhood to adulthood, when we became a woman or a man. If you recognize such a passage in your life, make some notes about it: Was it also a family rite of passage, or was it unique to the experiences of your life? Do you have a memento associated with it, a piece of jewelry or clothing or a photograph, or do you have a memory of an object or place that is no longer accessible to you? Make a catalog of notes about memories associated with this event that you know through each of the five senses. Before you write, read through your notes, then set them aside and write afresh from your heart, referring to the notes only occasionally to recapture a detail or phrase.

5. *Writing About Bad Things That Happened.* Coming to understand and accept the complexity of life can be difficult and daunting, even if nothing untoward happened to us. The betrayal of childhood is enough to warrant bitter memories. Sometimes that abstract betrayal is grounded in further, concrete betrayal: the betrayal of adults who were supposed to protect us, but instead hurt us. Such betrayal can take many forms, from the silence of neglect to the violence of sexual and physical abuse.

When writing about cruelties and tragedies of childhood and adolescence, it can help to identify strong images, objects or places that can serve as anchor for the painful and sometimes elusive memories. If images occur to you, trust them, and use them in your writing. If you find yourself unable to write about something that you do want to write about, try writing in the third person, *she* or *he*. Tell the story as though it is something you watched or that happened to someone else, because in some ways it did.

If you uncover memories, events or moments that you find especially disturbing or frightening, talk about them to someone you trust, and read books about child neglect, abuse and molestation. There is help now for claiming and understanding harmful experiences that we had as children and as adolescents. While we cannot change what was done, we can change how we know it and how we hold it in our memories. Then, perhaps, we can reconsider writing about it— or not writing about it. The choice is our own.

6. Other Experiments. Refer to the experiments in chapter two and chapter four, and use the techniques described there to write about your teenage years.

Writing About Adult Life

Our memories from childhood and adolescence tend to come in snippets—pictures and moments that are self-contained and can be approached through copious description. In a way, they are stories from past lives that now we only experience through memory: Our childhood and adolescence are over. Our adult lives, on the other hand, are ongoing, even though parts of them have concluded, and even though we change and might come of age—come to a new awareness of our selves and of life—many times.

Because our adult stories are not over, it can help, when writing about an episode in our adult lives, to write about a particular era that has a recognizable ending or to write about an episode that is self-contained.

Writing About a Period of Time

Writing about a period of time is a common way of presenting memory. There is a beginning, middle and end, the literary holy trinity that brings closure not only for the reader but for the writer as well. A memory is plucked out of the marathon of adult life, and is given shape and meaning. If I were to look for such episodes in my life, I would quickly arrive at these: the time I lived in Michigan; the time I lived in Ohio; graduate school; the period when we lived in town, before moving to the country.

When writing about these time periods, you can cast your personal experience into the light of the larger experience of society—the community, the country, the planet. For the writer, researching and describing the political, economic and other factors of the day can yield new consciousness of the episode under discussion. For example, my first marriage started to change the same year humans walked on the moon for the first time. The moon walk was a small step for man and a giant step for mankind, said astronaut Neil Armstrong as he stepped onto the surface of that alien land. And my awakening, not so much from marriage as from extended adolescence, marked a small change in my daily routine and a giant change in my life. I might not have thought about it that way had I not thought about what was going on in the world at that time.

Placing my story in a larger context also helps my readers. It places the episode in a historical context, and it offers them a way to relate it to their own lives, to times when they have taken giant steps.

You can also place an episode in the context of family events: "The year we moved to Montana was the year my baby sister was born." Sometimes personal and social contexts can be blended: "The year of the failed comet Kahoutec was the year my sister was born. The comet was a dud, but my sister screamed brightly through the sky of our family's life."

Writing About a Place

A geographical or physical place—a town or a house, for example—offers a comfort similar to the comfort of the beginning, middle and end of a time sequence. A place has boundaries, limits that can be mapped literally and figuratively. The house I lived in as a child was located at the crossing of Seventy-third Street and Emerson Avenue. The front yard sloped downward and tumbled into the backyard of the family next door. My life there tumbled forward, too, and did not slow down until the year we moved away, the year I turned thirteen.

There is also a chronological context for such places. In every place on Earth something happened, or did not happen, before our time. Writing about such facts or possibilities reveals the history of the land and can also reveal the meaning or value of our personal histories. Here's a little piece I wrote about my first home. While in some ways it is about childhood, the point of the story is more about adulthood—about an adult looking back at childhood.

Richfield

Anyone looking at a map of Richfield, Minnesota, would call it a suburb of Minneapolis, although it is a city in its own right. When I lived there it was technically a village. I didn't know that, of course. Government boundaries are of no use to children.

We drew our maps with different lines: St. Martin's backyard, Newquist's driveway and the abandoned dirt road behind Colbert's house. We called it Crookety Lane. It was our access to Wood Lake, a small, mud-bottomed slough hemmed in by hills and cattails and canary grass. It was there we learned about boundaries.

They were clearly recorded, not on paper, but in our hearts.

At Wood Lake, we hid from strangers, from each other and even from ourselves. We learned about small deaths there, when the law that was, after all, wilderness yielded up the corpses of birds and mice and fishes. And we became friends there, singing down the sun and walking home close together, the glow of our certitude holding back the impending dark.

I liked the clarity of that miniature world. When scrutinized, it revealed internal depths: the skin bone of a shrew, a snail's trail along primeval slime. But I was called, too, by the world up the hill, the one with streets that had names, and led one way to open fields and the other to the city.

It was my grandparents who showed me those streets. On Sunday afternoons, they came and got me and drove me away from home. I sat in the back seat, rubbing my hands on the maroon velvet. We scouted for land. My grandfather was a builder of houses. He built the one I lived in and the ones over on Diamond Lake Road. We drove over there sometimes and scanned the yards.

But most of the time we headed straight for the country. The houses thinned out and finally disappeared. Fields took over, rich fields, and the sky became longer and wider. The sun hung high forever and sometimes I wondered if we would ever go home.

Every childhood is interrupted by the coming-of-age of the human body. I was doubly wrested from youth. The year I was thirteen, we moved. Still, it was anticlimax. The year before, Patty's parents had taken her away, and Kippy's took her the year before that. Only Lottielee and Diane remained. None of us had been down to the lake for a long time, and for another, longer time, I forgot about Wood Lake. I followed the streets my grandparents showed me, paths that went farther away than any of us imagined they could. Finally, I went back to visit.

Riding in from the airport, I drove by houses nailed to land I remembered as fields, glowing and golden in Sunday sun. And I went to Wood Lake. Now it is a nature reserve, drained of its center by the dry life of the city and gathered inside the folds of a chain-link fence. I walked in there. Grasses grew where water had been.

I had changed, too. I sat a while then, on a bench on a boardwalk that reached to the middle of the lake bed. Ducks had come down once right where I was sitting. I closed my eyes, heard the quiver of their wings as they conned their landing. It matched perfectly the beating of my heart.

The story has a double context: It is about a period of time, viewed from another time, and it is also about a place. The layering perhaps accommodates the complexity of the experience for both the writer and the reader. The old place and time meld into the present place and time. Both nest into memory like nesting dolls, each one a thing in itself, yet made more precious by the doll it holds and the doll that holds it.

Writing About Travel

Travel writing has built-in chronology and place. Most trips start and end, and they go somewhere and come back to somewhere. These are skeletal facts, but if they are the story itself, the writing is likely to feel bare-boned to both the writer and reader. The context and shaping of travel stories comes not so much from the coming and going, but from the *being*—the being of the journey, of the destination and of the return home.

As with travel itself, writing about travel holds potential danger. I call it You Had to Be There Syndrome. Most of us have experienced this phenomenon when telling a story or joke that we found particularly amusing. We know it has happened when our audience stares at us with pained eyes, and all we get in verbal response is a forced "ha-ha" or "well, uh—that's interesting." To save ourselves and our listeners, we mutter in return, "I guess you had to be there."

The task of the travel writer, then, is to take the reader along on the journey. As with most writing, this is accomplished through the use of sensory detail— things we know through the five senses; the use of imagery—things the reader can picture in the mind's eye; and analogy or comparison—the placement of experiences in a larger, or sometimes parallel, context.

Here is an essay I wrote about a trip my husband and I took to Kenya to see the animals at home.

The Animals at Home

In Samburu, in Kenya, in East Africa, in the morning
the animals get up from their beds in the dry hills and

begin their walk to the Oasa Nyiro river. At the lodge at Samburu, we too wake up, have tea and coffee, and climb, half asleep into the safari van.

In just a few minutes drive, we are between the animals and the river. The animals do not mind. "That is because they have work to do," says our driver, Abu. "They must eat, and they must get to the river to drink." He guides the van along one vein of the network of half-roads that web the bush country of Samburu. When we come to a herd of elephants off to our right, he stops the van and turns off the engine.

Bill and I stand up, our heads and shoulders poking through the open top of the van, and look out across the bush. The elephants stroll along eating mostly dry grass. They grasp a clump with the tips of their trunks and then kick at the base with one foot, freeing grass and roots from the hard ground.

Today we watch a herd of thirty tembo. We stand silently in our metal viewing box, elbows to rooftop, and listen to them scuffling in the dirt. When they get closer, they part and go around us, the way water flows around rock. In soft voices, we say, "hello, hello tembo," and "hello toto, baby tembo." In fifteen minutes they have moved past us.

We move on, too, stopping again for twiga the giraffe and punda the zebra, for the antelope families, dik-dik and gerenuk, gazelle, oryx and impala, waterbuck and kudu. All graze like cows, following the smell of water to the river. By noon they will be there. They will drink, and then rest, and then will turn around and stroll back to the hills for the night.

It is not so different from home, where we also rise in the morning to go to work and return again, with the human herd, back to the hearth for the evening. It is quieter here, though. The guinea fowl move silently from the morning shade into the morning sun and out of the midday sun into the midday shade. The wind does not seem to blow, as though held in check by the equality of light and dark. Even my little human heart relaxes, the way a restless child does when it lays its head on the breast of the mother.

In addition to describing the event in detail, I place it in context: I compare a day in the life of an animal to the day in the life of a human. They have work to do, as we do; they return home in the evening, as we do.

I did not, however, think of that comparison before I wrote this piece. It emerged for me as I wrote. The early simple comparison of "They have work to do," given to me by our driver, Abu, set up the notion in my mind that I capitalized on in the last paragraph. As is so often true, my instinct to record a certain detail offered me an idea or a form that I used to take my readers by the hand so they could be there with me.

Holidays, Family Gatherings and Other Special Events

Most of us have family or neighborhood stories that we tell over and over again at gatherings: the day Aunt Gertie got a speeding ticket, the time the dogs ate the Thanksgiving turkey, the Halloween night when Barb and Myron scared the kids who were playing in the barn.

When we tell these tried-and-true tales, everyone laughs and contributes—or contradicts—details. These stories become well polished in the retelling, and in our hearts they feel rich and full. But when we try to write them down they often fall flat: You had to be there.

The stories seem rich and full to us when we tell them out loud because our listeners usually know the circumstances in which the events of the stories took place. The task of the writer is to uncover the elements of the circumstances that contribute to the mood and meaning of the events, and bring them to the writing. It is done in the usual way: sensory details, images, analogies. The first step is to recognize that strangers, our readers, do not have the circumstances of the original event. The second step is to provide it for them.

Writing about stories that are oft retold is not quite the same thing as writing about the social gatherings where the stories are retold. However, the methods for bringing the gatherings to life, for bringing the reader to the table, are the same: sensory detail, image and analogy.

Here are two stories of mine. The first, "Lighting the Way," is about a family holiday tradition. The second, "Toads," is a neighborhood memory. I remember writing both of them: As the details revived for me with the writing, I let myself revel in them, let them tell the stories.

Lighting the Way

Dinner had been over for a long time. It had been dark outside, it seemed, forever. I returned to Grandmother's dining room once more to see if the grown-ups had finished their endless cups of coffee. Slipping over to the bay window behind the table, I stared out at the neighborhood lights and waited for the right moment.

In the living room the other kids were still fussing over a board game. Drowsy and a little crabby from the surfeit of good food, they seemed to have forgotten that the best part of Thanksgiving was yet to come.

I turned away from the window and leaned against my mother.

"Mahhhh-mm."

"OK, OK."

My mother shifted in her chair. At last the departure had begun. I hustled importantly back into the living room. My siblings hadn't missed me, but they would pay attention now.

"We're getting ready to go. Put everything away. Come on. Let's go. Come ON. We're going downtown to see the lights."

The lights. That was what Thanksgiving really meant. The turning on of the Christmas lights in downtown Minneapolis. Before long the seven of us were packed into the car, doors slammed and locked, and then we coasted in our quiet basket from the sparse suburbs toward the worst traffic jam of the year.

As we got closer to downtown, the cars arranged themselves in long ropes, their headlights and tail-lights festooning the streets. I liked being one of those lights, strung out in the middle of the city dark like that, lighting the way to Christmas.

Christmas, for me, was largely a matter of lights. In

the morning on the school bus, I breathed open a space in the frosted window and looked for the houses that turned on their trees for breakfast, the way I did. And at night I went into a dark room, and leaned into the window to see who in the neighborhood had remembered and who had forgotten to plug in their lights. Sometimes I just sat in our own living room with all of the other lights off to see what I could see in just the glow from the Christmas tree.

There is a special quality to that light. It illumines the heart of the house, the way the downtown lights illumine the heart of the city. By its glow, whether at home or out, we can see how rich and full light itself can be, and we are, for a moment, fuller and richer of heart ourselves.

Gradually the traffic slowed and then almost stopped. Downtown buildings showed themselves, and finally, we were on the main street itself. Ahead and overhead garlands of lights lifted in endless repetition linking building to building, street to street, and the hearts of children to each other's hearts, and the hearts of grown-ups to their own childhood hearts.

It was almost a relief when we reached the end of the arch, and our heavy boat turned away from the stream and drifted down the long, black aisles of the other side of the city. I closed my eyes then and let myself fall asleep against the shoulders of my brothers and sisters, playing back the reel of color, of contrast, of hope against darkness.

Toads

We don't know where the toads came from. We only remember that one day in the spring or summer, when we were all grade-school age, they appeared in great numbers, emerging from the dirt cut bank alongside the dirt road that ran between my house and St. Martin's. There may have been only dozens of them, but in my memory there were hundreds. They were less than one inch long, and they never stopped moving, and we children of the neighborhood played with them the way we played with dolls.

In the side of the same hill from which they emerged, with our stubby fingers, we scooped holes and built mud fences and tried to keep the little toads inside them. They clambered up and out of the pens, spilling into each other's houses and sometimes rolling down the steep pitch of the cut bank, landing on our bare feet. We scooped them up in our little hands, and returned them to the sweet homes we'd made for them and for which they were utterly ungrateful.

It seems to me the toad outbreak lasted only one day. When we came back the second day, they were gone, dispersed into the tangle of vines that grew out of one end of the cut bank, or the other way, up to where the bank leveled off at the top of the hill and met St. Martin's yard. Maybe some of them even made it down the street and into the vacant lot, and then down to the swamp and lake behind Mrs. Walters's house.

Eventually, we children, too, found our way out of the neighborhood, outgrowing the reach of our parents' hands and seeking homes of our own making. But the memory of those toads stays with me—their abundance, their simplicity, their persistent drive to escape from our clumsy clutches.

What was it in us that made us want to own them?

What was it in them that refused to be owned?

Experiments

1. Writing About a Certain Period of Time. Try marking your adult life into two or more passages: I lived in this city from this year to that year; I worked in one career from age twenty-two to thirty-three; I cared for my mother for nine months—the same amount of time she carried me.

Write a few paragraphs or pages about each period. What else was going on at the time, in your family, in your community, in the world?

2. Writing About Place. Make a list of places in your life for which you have strong memories: a town, a church building, a house, a neighborhood. Choose one or two and develop some history for them: Who or what was there before you were? How do your experiences there confirm or contradict the history of the place?

3. Writing About Travel. A trip can be to a distant place or to a near one. I remember a day trip that our Camp Fire girl group took when I was about eight. I also remember a trip to Africa I took just a few years ago. Both have meaning for me. Make a list of some journeys you have taken, whether they are near or far.

For some of them, the ones that call to you in some way, try to think of things that "you had to be there" to know or understand. Then ask yourself why you had to be there. Those details are usually prefaced in note-making with "I don't know, it was just sort of, well, you know—the sounds, the smells." Record as many sensory details as you can remember.

4. *Writing About Faith or Spirituality.* When we talk about faith or spirituality, we often turn to abstractions. We have faith, hope and charity; we are prayerful or fearful or stand in awe. Perhaps we turn to the abstract because spirit is something we cannot see or touch. Still, in order to express our feelings and beliefs, we can turn to the concrete, to sensory images. This is perhaps why the cross, something we can see and touch, is a symbol for Christianity, why Jews light their menorahs and why Buddha is made manifest in joyful statues.

If you wish to write about your faith, look for images that express for you the values and the feelings of your belief. The flame of a candle might represent spirit; a shawl might represent the comfort of faith; a book might represent the wisdom of your religion. As you tell the story of the object, relate the object to your feelings: As you hold the book in your hands, so you hold the wisdom of the ancestors in your heart.

5. *Providing Context for the Reader.* Besides vivid re-creation of the scene, one way to provide the context of a family story for the reader, who is a stranger, is to think and write about the meaning of the story. Most stories we retell have a subtle message in them—a message about folly or courage or hope or failure. Make a list of several stories that are told over and over again at neighborhood picnics or at the family table. Using the trilogy of questions discussed in chapter six, seek out the values expressed in the stories.

CHAPTER FIVE

Interviews and Research

Much of the material we need for a memoir we carry in our heads and hearts. By definition, the memoir is composed of memories—our memories. A full-bodied memoir, however, is likely to reach beyond the bounds of our personal experience. It will likely place our experience in the perspective of the times, places and people of the original moments.

Doing research, looking for information outside of our memories, can also inspire refreshed memories, and fuller ones. When I get together with my siblings, I am always surprised at how much more I remember about an incident as we each spin out our version of it. "Do you remember . . . " is a common phrase during such conversations, and to my surprise, I do remember—that cookie jar, the dead-end alley off Oak Grove, the house on Lyndale we thought was haunted. Without the stimulus of our group recollection, many such memories might stay forever in the dark basement of my singular memory.

Searching for resources outside our own memories can also provide new information—information that we did not have at the time of the experience we'll write about. It might be statistical, historic or geographic, and it might help place experiences in a larger societal context.

When I am preparing to research a period of time in

my life, I like to do it before I do any writing. However, I usually end up doing additional research during the process of my writing because questions emerge that I did not think of beforehand. Some writers, however, commit words and thoughts to paper first, and then look for material to enhance what they've written. Others write, research, write, research in an in-and-out fashion. There is no singular correct way to bring light to your material: Work in a way that is successful for you.

Interviews

Interviewing people is, for me, one of the joys of doing research. I love the unexpected treasures that are revealed through a visit with someone over a cup of tea. And I like that interviews can happen any time, any place, without notice and without real intent.

If you are working on a memoir, it is a good idea to keep a small tablet and pen with you at all times, especially when you will be around people who might have something to tell you about the time or place you are writing about. The best interviews sometimes happen spontaneously, at the dinner table over a holiday meal or during an after-dinner walk.

Perhaps spontaneous interviews work so well because they arise out of a moment of common conversation: You and the other person are part of some social event, and the subject you are writing about has risen naturally from a general discussion. When this happens, you can, without much notice, elicit more information. If Auntie says, "Well, that's the way Unc was, you know," you can ask for more. "What did Unc do for a living? Why was he like that?'' Or, ''Did you and Unc always live near each other?'' If it seems appropriate, you could quickly find paper and pencil and make sketchy notes, or you can rely on your memory. Often the information you get that will be useful to you will not be specific details, but rather a sense of the way things were. Later, you can sit down and replay the conversation in your head, and make full notes about it.

If you set up a formal interview—if you make an appointment with someone, for example—there are a few protocols you might honor. These are not rules, really, but they can help the interview go more smoothly, and help you and your interviewee get into the subject you want to hear about.

First, tell your interviewee why you want to talk to them. You might have done this when you set up the interview, but it is a good idea to go through it again when you meet. It helps set a tone for the interview, and lets your subject know how their information will be used.

At the same time, tell them what you will give them in return for their help. The standard recompense is a copy of the book. I also offer additional copies at a discount, so my interviewees can purchase them to use as gifts. Write down whatever you offer, because it is easy to forget such details. I use the interview worksheet on page 54 for all formal interviews.

If you want to use a tape or video recorder, you should ask for permission first, and do not assume that you will get it. Your subject is doing you a favor, and you want them to feel comfortable. If you do use such

Name of interviewee:

Date of interview:

Referred to me by:

Title, organization, relationship, etc.:

Phone:

Fax:

E-mail:

Offered in compensation:

Other promises made:

Interview notes:

equipment, try to minimize its presence. And whether or not you use equipment, take notes.

I am an advocate of written notes over recorded notes. First, if you record a three-hour interview and don't make notes, you have to listen to the whole thing again and transcribe it. This is not a pleasant task. Second, the recorder only records what was said. It does not note questions or make side comments. That is for you to do—on your notepad.

Taking notes also adds a personal touch to the interview, and includes the interviewee in a way that recording equipment does not. The interviewee will probably be interested in your notes. You can take time to stop and say, "Uh—I didn't quite get that—did you say. . . ." This allows for clarification or return to a comment and further discussion of it. Sometimes when I'm interviewing I'll read something from my notes out loud: "You said, '_____.' That's such an interesting take on the experience. How did you come to such wisdom?"

Handwritten notes are also easier to refer to when you are actually writing your memoir. It is easier to thumb through papers than to forward through a tape recording.

When you are done with the interview, ask your subject to please call you if they think of anything else they'd like to tell you. Give them your number, and be sure to ask if you can contact them again if you need to clarify something in your notes or if you think of something else.

Before you go to an interview, do some thinking about the subject yourself. Make notes about why you're going to talk to this person and what you hope to find out from them. And make a list of questions that you can use to move the conversation along should it falter. They might be very specific questions, such as, "What was the address of your first house?" or general questions, such as, "What was Grandmother like when she was a girl?"

While such a list helps you prepare for an interview and is a good safety net, use it cautiously. Usually we conduct an interview to find out what we do not know. You might use one or two questions to get the interview underway, but if at all possible, from then on you should let the interviewee determine the direction of the conversation. Ask questions about what was just said, and look for opportunities to connect comments to your own questions, rather than just asking your questions one after the other.

"Suzie was one of my best childhood friends. We walked to school together every day."

"What school did you go to? Was it the one at the corner of Penn and Sixty-eighth?"

or

"Were there a lot of children in the neighborhood?"

or

"What did your mother do while you were in school?"

If you let your interviewee lead the conversation, it is not likely to progress in the order of your questions, but it is more likely to lead to something you did not know.

The first five minutes of an interview is usually the

most awkward part. You can soften it by leading gradually into your subject. After you've restated your need for the interview and offered a book in return for the favor, you can talk about the place you are in before you get to your subject: "This garden is beautiful—how long have your cared for it?" Or, "This is a long way from the house you and Mom grew up in—how long have you lived here?"

You can also use props to help the interview get underway. You might bring a photograph that your subject can talk about or a memento—a candy dish, a map, or a news clipping. During the interview, you can also ask if your interviewee has pictures or mementos. "She would be my great-grandmother, then. Do you have a picture of her?" The picture might inspire more memories—and more questions.

I have a favorite closing question that I use for all interviews: "Is there something about this that other people just don't seem to understand?" This question works well at the end of an interview because many facets of the subject have been raised, and it gives your interviewee a chance to put things in perspective.

After you leave the interview, try to find time to write about it. Make notes on how it went, what you learned and what new questions it raised. If it made you want to talk to more people, write down their names and some questions you might ask them. If you came away with mementos—a photograph, for example—make note of who you got it from and why it is important. It might be months before you will use your new information and, although you are writing from memory, these new memories might not have the staying power of the old ones.

Research

Library research is an interview without the personal contact. Details and perceptions are locked away in paper and electronic files, and it is your job to lure them out of hiding. As with interviews, you will often learn more if you follow leads that are revealed to you rather than only following a predetermined path.

When I do research, I look for printed materials that might help me understand my subject. If you have not been in a library for a while, you might be surprised to discover that the old card catalogs no longer exist. They have been replaced with electronic catalogs. Once you get used to using a computer catalog, your nostalgia for the old way will disappear quicker than fog on a summer morning. If you don't know how to use a computer catalog, just ask someone. Librarians are usually glad to help you become proficient with this wonderful technology.

Computer catalogs allow you to search your topic in several ways, including by subject, title or author. You can search for books, articles, government documents and other forms of information. You type in the words you want the computer to search for, and it comes back with a list of items. Usually you can print out this list and use it for browsing the stacks.

Some computer catalogs are also online catalogs. An in-house computer library exists only in the building that houses the computer. An online library catalog is maintained on a Web site, which can be accessed from home or from anywhere in the world. Ask your local librarian for information on accessing online library catalogs.

To search for books that might not be in libraries, go to an online bookstore such as http://www.amazon.com or http://www.barnesandnoble.com. You can search by topic, title or author. If you find something you want, you can order it online, or you can ask your library to order it for you through interlibrary loan.

Unless you are very familiar with library research, it is a good idea to talk to a librarian about your project. There may be resources in your library, such as genealogy records and government documents, that you don't know about.

When doing your library research, don't forget to check out newspapers from the time period you are interested in. You will probably have to learn to load microfilm and microfiche machines, but don't let that stop you. Reading the news of the day from the year you were born or started high school can give you fresh insights into your life that other sources might not offer.

Public Records

Most public records of land and life (birth, deaths) are kept in county courthouses. You have the right to access many of these records. To find out what is available to you and how to access it, call or visit your county courthouse. Someone there will help you find what you are looking for. You might also find records in city, town and township offices.

The Internet

Although library catalogs are now kept on in-house computers or online, searching them is not the same as searching the Internet. Library catalogs contain information on library holdings. An Internet search yields listings of Web sites available through the Internet. Unlike library holdings, which exist in a building somewhere, Internet Web sites exist only in the electricity of a *server*, a computer component that handles large amounts of data and is connected to other servers through telephone lines.

If you do not already use the Internet (also called the Web or the World Wide Web), ask someone to show it to you. Most teenagers today are adept at using this technology, and letting them help you is a way to connect with them. You do not have to own a computer to use the Internet. Public libraries have taken up the call, and most have Internet terminals with free access for their patrons. Often they also offer classes on Internet use, as do community education offices.

The biggest challenge with searching the Internet is not finding a lot of information, but rather with limiting and selecting the massive amount of information that is available. You can limit your search by using advanced search techniques. These are a little bit different for each *search engine*, the technology used to accomplish the search. Do not be shy: Click on the help button and learn how to sharpen your search.

Once you have searched for a topic and narrowed it down, you will still want to evaluate the Web sites that you find. They may be put up by the kid down the street, by someone in another country or by your local government. Anyone can put up a Web site. Your concern will be the validity of the information that you find. Even a professional-looking Web site can contain false or biased information.

To judge the integrity of a Web site, you can look for several things.

- Is it presented by a well-known entity, such as a university or a corporation?
- Does it claim and show evidence of a board of directors, who you are able to contact?
- Does it present unbiased information? Many Web sites have a special agenda—they want to present their point of view only. This is valid for them, but might not be for your research.
- Can you find information on other sites or in traditional print sources that confirm the information on the site in question?

You can enter most Web sites free of charge. Be extremely cautious about a site that asks for a credit card number to obtain entry. Also be careful about purchasing items over the Web. If you want to do that, talk to someone you trust who understands Web commerce before you use a credit card online.

If you want to purchase online but also want to protect your credit, you might obtain a credit card and ask for a low limit on it, such as five hundred dollars. The low limit helps protect your credit from being compromised.

Never give anyone your social security number, checking account or other such numbers online.

Using Interviews and Research Materials

Interviews and research are labor-intensive activities that might not seem to yield a high return. Often, most often perhaps, you will not use more than a tidbit here and there in your memoir. But do not discount the effort and the gain. Reading and hearing about broad aspects of your life, aspects you were not even aware of at the time, ultimately do affect what you write and how you write it. Your writing will take on an authority that it might not have if you rely only on your personal memory.

In addition to affecting your writing, contacts with other people and research activity can turn up illustrative sources for your book: pictures, maps, news clippings, a concert program. Added to similar items from your own closet, these visual renditions of your experience add another dimension to your memoir. They offer the reader a break from the words and time to contemplate what they have read.

Illustrative materials offer another advantage to the book: You can use the captions to present information that does not easily fit into your text. The caption for a picture of Main Street might include population statistics or a comment on the difference between the street then and now. The caption under a birth certificate might afford the opportunity to say what became of the hospital you were born in.

Experiments

1. Self-Interview. While it can be enlightening to interview other people for your book, it can also be illuminating to interview yourself. If you've written questions to use in your interviews, try answering them yourself. Write out your responses so you can refer to them later.

2. *Home-Base Research.* Local libraries often have special sections on the community, including clipping files, as well as books by local authors and copies of newspapers that no longer exist. As you prepare to write your memoir, visit the library of its locale. Ask about special collections, including local history and genealogy.

3. *Web Search.* Using an Internet search engine, search for sites that have the name of your town or local attractions, such as a lake or park. Search for your own name. Search for information on memoirs. You will find much that is of no interest to you, but you might also find something you would come across no other way. Perhaps someone else has a Web site on your town, or perhaps your cousin three times removed has a site that includes family history.

4. *Web Presence.* Consider putting up your own Web site about your memoir. See chapter ten for more on this subject.

CHAPTER SIX

Discovering Values in your Writing

The telling of stories is at least as old as the tribal camp-fire. In stories we commiserate, we enlighten, we instruct. We pass along traditions and secure history. We ask questions and conjure up answers.

The memoir, perhaps the original storytelling genre, is popular today. With the turn of the millennium and the rise of technology, both of which threaten to separate us from our pasts, maybe we find comfort in the stories of our personal lives and in the preservation of our histories. But I think something else is at work here, too: I think that when we write our pasts, we also write the present and the future. The act of writing, of giving voice to our experiences, thoughts and feelings, changes how we are in the moment and how we move forward. When the past is securely nailed to the page, we can use it as an anchor while we adventure into the rest of our lives, even into the unfathomable twenty-first century.

Writing about our lives also offers us the opportunity to put experiences, events and emotions in perspective. Writing about portions of our lives can frame them the way a picture frame embraces a work of art: It both limits the picture and sets it off.

Framing a work of art changes it in other ways as

well: The frame assumes an audience, someone who looks at the art for what it is, separate from its creation or its value to the artist. Frames in writing fold in upon themselves: We frame an experience by telling the story, and we frame the story by relaying not only the facts of it, but its value to us and others.

Such notions, however, are not usually the inspiration for the writing of a memoir. Most of us come to it from an intuitive sense. We say to ourselves, "I should write about that," or someone else might say it to us. Such spontaneous instruction is the proper beginning for any writing. The American poet Robert Frost said a poem is never born thought-first, and I think that is true of most writing. Something wells up in the heart and asks, sometimes demands, to be spoken.

Once the writing is underway—the telling of a time, or a place, or an event, or a person in your life—once you have started framing your life into stories, opportunities arise for framing the meanings and values of the stories themselves. Because literary frames are made of words and not of wood, they may be woven through a story the way a contrasting thread may be woven through fabric, or they may open a story, a gateway of sorts, or close it off.

Uncovering Meaning and Value

When we start to write we might not be aware of the meanings or values in the stories we tell, but we almost certainly know them somewhere in our minds or hearts, else we would not have the desire to write them. The task therefore is not to assign value and meaning to our stories, but to uncover the values and meanings expressed in them.

I have a trick I use to reveal to myself the sometimes hidden meanings and values that underpin memories I want to write about. I ask myself a series of three questions about the memory: (1) What is my purpose in writing about it? (2) What is the overall theme? (3) What values are expressed in the telling of the story? I do this before I write, and I make notes about my answers and try to elaborate on them. When it is time to write the story, I set my notes aside so they will inform my thinking about the story but will not limit the writing of it. Notes such as these describe what a reader might infer from the story, but they are not the story itself.

When I ask myself what my purpose is in writing the story, I try to keep my answer simple. Perhaps I just want to record a memory. Perhaps I want my own children to come to know the grandmother who died years before they were born. Perhaps I want to preserve for myself and for others a sense of a certain place. I do not strive to justify the desire, only to name it: "I feel like writing about the day my first child was born."

When I ask myself what the subject of the story might be, I usually use some of the same words I used in describing my purpose. In the story proposed previously, simply put, the subject is the birth of my first son. Or it could be the birthing of my son, which is different in subtle ways from his birth, as it is more about me than about him. Both of these notions, however, are still narrowly focused on the major event of the story. When I think about "subject" I try to expand it to "theme." If this story were to be placed in an anthology, what themes might it be placed under? Now the possibilities expand: the beginning of life, the rite of passage into motherhood, physical trials of the female body, turning points in adult life. I write down everything I think of.

The third question, what values are expressed in the story and by the fact of the story, also turns on the words I used in the first two questions, but adds the context of value. The writing of a birth story, I might say, implies that birthing is an important event—it is valued and has meaning. Or it might imply that carrying on a family line is important or that the blending of two souls into one is a good thing. If the birth had gone awry, I might have wanted to say that the loss of a child, even one you do not know yet, is tragic.

This discovery sequence can even be applied outside of writing, to ordinary or extraordinary life events. I teach college writing, and at the beginning of a term, I sometimes ask my students why they are in school. I get many answers, including these: to get an education, to get started in a career, to bide time until I know what I want to be when I grow up.

Then I ask them to name some overall subjects or themes related to education—what is education about, in a general way? Their answers usually include knowledge, skills, opportunities, social interactions and growing independence. Then I ask them to uncover the values implied in the purposes and themes they listed. What is implied that is good? Or bad? Knowledge is good; lack of knowledge is bad. Skills are good; lack of skills is bad.

My trilogy does not contain new ideas. We often use similar methods, for example, to evaluate people and places. We might infer from a person's spiffy clothing that they value neatness or cleanliness, and from the chaos of a child's room that the child does not. Capacious parks in a city imply that the community values nature and leisure time.

While the trilogy is useful for thinking about a topic, I do not find it useful as a form for writing. Rather, I use it as a way to bring my topic more clearly into focus and to cast it in a larger context. After I have completed my exercise, I set my notes from it aside. The purpose was to call forward in my mind ideas and words that might help me write my story more fully. In a way, it is a warm-up to the work. Musicians run scales and chords before they play at a performance. A carpenter moves lumber and nails and tools to the building site. Artists set out paints and prepare canvas. Thinking about my story in terms of purpose, theme and value brings my materials together in one place: my head.

Where You Work

Your work space might begin to feel cluttered after a while. You've got all these ideas sitting about on your desk, along with the images and concrete, sensory details that I described in chapters two and three. How can you write with such a mess in your way? It is not so different, though, from other processes we engage in. When we go to church, we pass through heavy doors into a space defined by color and light and texture. As we enter, the concerns of the outer world fall away, and we accept with some ease the concerns of an inner world. We do the same thing when we go to a party or a picnic. We prepare by gathering around us what we will need: food, drink, bug spray, blankets. Some things we'll use, others not, but at least they are handy. And some of the most important things we did as part of our preparation are not visible at all. I don't make mayonnaise salads for picnics for fear of salmonella poisoning. I value a safe, healthy meal and a good time uninterrupted by bad food.

In fact, most of the time the words and ideas from my notes do not appear directly in my writing. Instead, they are invisible but can be inferred. Here is a short essay I wrote about my mother.

Lessons

One of my strongest memories of my mother is of the two of us down at the lake, at the end of the dock. She did not go there often; she spent most of her time in the house. But I remember one day. It was calm. The lake had all the steamy smells of the season: algae, fish, gasoline. There was no wind. The water spread itself out like a baby blue blanket, waiting to swaddle us.

I was a teenager, fifteen years old. I let myself into the water, wincing at the cold that slipped over me like a glove. My mother sat down on the edge of the dock and dangled her feet in the water. Although she had her swimsuit on, nothing I said could get her to leave the warm harbor of sunlit air. I did not understand. I tried to convince her that she would like it, and I believed I was right. She demurred still and I felt unhappy for her.

It was my first lesson in aging, but I did not learn it until many years later, at the ocean with my teenage son. He leaped into the waves, half porpoise, half man. "Come on," he called to me, "you'll like it, it's warm once you get in."

Once you get in. That's what I said to my mother. I scuffed along the beach staying just out of reach of the top scallop of the waves that ran up on the sand, mixing the warm grains with cool droplets. When I was fifteen I did not think about warm or cool. Things were either hot or cold, good or bad. And everything was reversible. If the water was cold, I swam hard and got warm. I didn't think about getting out of breath . . . sometimes I just felt like floating awhile or laying myself out on the dock like an abandoned fish. And then I didn't listen to my breath or feel a sinking in my chest. I knew only the sun working its way down layer by layer into my skin.

My son came up out of the ocean, the water dripping off his thin and happy body, and walked with me. I must be getting old, I said. I don't want to get wet. That's when I thought of my mother on the dock. She had swirled her feet around now and then, making little waves that came out to me, but mostly she had leaned back on her arms, closed her eyes and let the sun work on her face.

Now I know that the glare under her eyelids blotted out the piles of laundry on the basement floor, the mending in the basket by her chair and the mental note to herself to take something out of the freezer for dinner. Except for my nagging, she had a peaceful moment in the sun.

Neither of us knew it then, but my mother was dying of cancer. Aging for her would be accelerated. She died three years later. That was a lesson, too, and another one I did not learn until many years later, when my younger son died.

Aging has many facets. It is a kaleidoscope: The slightest movement forces a different picture. Sometimes the body leads, sometimes the mind. Sometimes circumstance passes through the peephole with the severity of a star gone nova. Gradually we learn which way to hold our heads, when to look up, when to look down, when to close our eyes and wait.

I hope I do not have to hurry into death. I need the time to become stronger. I have decided I will be strong. I have an image of myself as an old woman. I am unsure of the body, but I know the spirit: It is infused with a sense of well-being; it is a magnate that draws me toward it. As I get closer to it, I shed the skin that is my body. I become careless of it, have little use for it.

Sometimes I can hardly wait: I can feel the sun working on my face. My feet dangle in cool water. The breeze comes up and unlocks my heart.

What was my purpose in writing this story? For me, it was to think past a simple memory of my mother and to discover some larger meaning about her or about our relationship.

Subjects or themes: mothers, mothers and daughters, aging, death.

Values expressed: It is good to understand our lives and how we are with each other; aging is not to be feared.

I might not have been able to infer all of these notions prior to writing the story, but trying to find them, seeking a larger context for my experience before I write, makes it easier for me to create a larger context in the writing. And when I also use the questions to look for such context in work after it is written, I am able to understand better what I have said and what my readers might get from my work. Sometimes my answers inspire revision.

Pencil to Paper

Thinking about writing is the easy part. It is pencil to paper that tasks the mind and soul. Often someone says to me, "I've thought about writing my family story," and I say, "Good idea—don't wait to get started." I mean it, too, but I'm also thinking, "Yeah, we'll see how far you get when you come square up against a blank sheet of paper."

Writing is a daunting and dangerous task. When we mess with words, we mess with our lives and with ideas. It is also rewarding and empowering: Our word *authority* derives from the word *author*. Somehow we recognize this power when we sit down to write and suddenly, even though we have fought for the time and space to finally sit down with pencil and paper, we suddenly don't know what to say.

This is true of experienced writers as well as new ones. For me, the most exciting and most awful part of a writing project is the moment I sit down to start it. The landscape of the blank page lies open before me, ripe with possibility, and for a while all I can see is a void that wants to swallow me whole.

How to start then? Your story can be arranged chronologically or by some other criterion: places lived in; life passages, such as marriage, births, deaths, divorce; change in health; spiritual change. It can help to trust the images, the moments, that occur to you to write about, even if you don't understand them at the time. As you write, you might come to know why the memory surfaced for you—what your purpose is in writing about it, what its theme is, what values you express by remembering and writing it.

The Internal Censor

The pressure of choosing where and how to start your writing can be complicated by another factor: censorship. This is not the censorship of the external critic, but of the internal voice. Perhaps you have thought to write about something that is disturbing to you personally. Or perhaps you heard often as a child, as I did, "If you can't say something nice, don't say anything at all."

Don't say anything at all. What a sad commandment. I realized as an adult that I had taken it in whole. It did not mean to me simply, "Don't say bad things about other people; don't gossip." It meant don't inquire, don't challenge, don't explore. Don't tell the truth if the truth is not pretty.

I must claim responsibility for my overindulgence in the platitude. I don't believe it was imposed on me any more than "Don't talk with your mouth full" or "Cover your mouth when you yawn." I realize now, as I write these phrases that occur to me, that all three of them address concerns of the mouth.

How much courage it takes to speak our minds. But that, I think, is what we do when we write a memoir. We articulate, acknowledge and declare ourselves. We consider how we got to this place where we now stand, and we want others to consider it, too. With luck, our writings will help them know how they got to where they stand.

Taking Heart

The act of writing is so complex. I want to write freely, unconstrained by fear. But I also want to be fair. How do I tell the difference between honesty and revenge, between truth and retribution? It takes courage to struggle with this, and not just courage to tell the truth. It takes courage to recognize when we are telling the truth in order to get back at someone, to claim our pound of flesh. Such motives, I think, are contrary to art, including the art of the memoir.

If you are unsure about what you write, there is a fairly simple test that can help you evaluate your words: Would you be willing to say them to the face of the person, even if it was hard to do so? You might have to defend your reasons for feeling the way you do. Imagine the conversation. Listen to your reasons—listen for images and events and sensory details. Therein lies your story. Our word *courage* comes from the French *coeur*, "heart."

Take heart. Say something not nice.

Experiments

1. *What Does It Mean?* Just as it helps to practice playing piano or ball, it can help to practice thinking about your writing. In this chapter, I propose a set of three questions that can lead you to a larger under-standing of your work: (1) What is your purpose in writing? (2) What is the overall subject or theme of you work? (3) What values do you express? One way to practice using these questions is to apply them to a novel or poem you have read, a song you like, a conver-sation you participated in or overheard, or a family activity or event.

2. *Getting Started.* Getting started can be the hard-est part of a writing project. Fear is often behind our resistance: fear of what we might say, or not say; fear of what we might learn; fear of failure; fear of exposure. If you have trouble getting started with your writing, as most of us do, try naming some fears that might be holding you back. Once named, you can perhaps de-cide if you want to proceed, or not.

3. *Don't Say Anything at All?* Writing a memoir can be like opening the proverbial can of worms: Things might get out that you had not thought of before you started writing. Fortunately, the writing is yours, and you get to choose what to include and what to exclude. Sometimes it is easier to write if you decide some of these things ahead of time. For example, if I decide I want to write about a certain Christmas event, I might not want to include an unpleasant episode from the middle of the day. It's my choice. I could also decide to let that episode dominate my story. My choice.

Look at some of the writing you have already done or notes for writing you intend to do. You have almost certainly already made decisions about things to include and exclude. Identify them and reconsider them. Why did you make the choice you did? Are you satisfied with it?

If you are unsure, it can sometimes help to talk to someone you trust about your choices.

4. Writing About Difficult Emotions. It would be a rare life that did not contain struggles with difficult emotions and experiences. As with other writing, it can help to turn to images and concrete details when writing about such difficulties. And, of course, you can decide not to write about them or decide not to include them after you have written them. It is your story. You get to tell it the way you want.

CHAPTER SEVEN

Facing the Blank Page

It is fun to think about writing a book. When I am musing about it—when I am inspired by my personal muse—I feel the fullness of the story I have to tell. It has energy and meaning and value. The love I feel for my life and for those in my life overflows from the well of my heart.

These feelings are especially strong at times when I am not able to commit them to paper—when I am driving in the car, falling asleep at night, or telling a snippet of a story on the phone, or in conversation at the kitchen table. At those moments I am certain that I have something to say.

When the same story calls to me a number of times, I start making time in my head and my calendar for writing it down: three weekends from now my husband and I have no plans; I will get up on Saturday morning and go upstairs and will not balance my checkbook or call my sisters or rearrange the mess on my desk; I will start up my computer and will start my new story.

The weekend comes at last. I have turned down a luncheon engagement because I have promised myself that I will start my new book. I rise in the morning, full of expectation and not a little dread. I go upstairs to my computer, turn it on and open a new computer file. The blank page spreads out before me. It only needs to be filled in with the story I was so certain I had to tell.

I put my fingers to the keyboard, but already I know they will not move. As I settle down to my task, the one I myself chose, the one I worked hard to make space for, the original inspiration abandons me. The flood of good feeling and desire that washed over me so easily in the car or at the table or at the brink of sleep is replaced by a tinny, scrawny feeling of inadequacy. What made me think I could write this book?

I am not being disingenuous or crafty when I say this, even though I am in the middle of chapter seven of my tenth book. The difference between me and the novice writer who has a similar experience is that I know something about that horrible and hopeful moment when I begin something new: I know that I will break through my own silence and write the book.

That knowledge softens the despair of the moment, for I do know how to break the silence, at least for myself. My methods, however, are not the only ones. In the end, we must each discover for ourselves the rope that will pull us out of the void.

In searching for your way out of the void, it is important to understand, and to believe, that the story you once felt like telling is worth telling, and to understand that the problem of the moment is not the adequacy of the story but the fact that at the moment you are not in story land. You are at your desk. In order to reenter the mood you were in when you first wanted to write the story, you must leave your desk, figuratively, and reenter the feelings of the story itself.

Tips on Getting Started

I have several tricks that I use to lure myself away from the reality of my office. Sometimes I read some of my other work. If I have written an outline, proposal or notes about the book at hand, I read that. I stare out the window, think about the place I want to write about and conjure it in detail—the color of the grass, the smell of the dried leaves, the brick texture of the house next door.

Gradually, the feelings that inspired my desire to write begin to arise in me. My fingers move across the keyboard making lists: the names of all the children in the neighborhood, the names of the streets, the shape of the land. Then, sometimes, I am able to start writing. If not, I try another tack—I turn to my notes and reread them or start new notes on a new topic. Or I try to conjure the finished book, how big it is, what the cover looks like, who reads it. Sometimes, then, I can almost read from the finished pages and type them onto my screen. It feels a bit like cheating, but after all, the reverie is mine.

The creative act is so curious. It is conscious and unconscious. The intent that drives it can also limit it; the desire that fuels it can also drown it. Luckily, as we write, as we become more used to it and more skilled at it, we find our personal balance with these and other facets of the creative jewel.

You are likely to experience the development of your skills as you move forward with your project. You might finally have managed to force out a few pages of the first chapter of your book, when you had to stop. You come back to it a week later, and once again the muse drought is upon you. But this time, you have your previous pages to read. They help pull you into the story, and while you reread them you can fine-tune them. It will also be easier to get back into your work because you probably continue to think about it at odd times. But now, instead of just floating away, the energy of those thoughts funnel quite naturally into a reservoir that comes along with your writing.

Talking to yourself

Although writing is in some ways a mysterious skill, in other ways it is not. None of us would expect to play Bach perfectly on the piano after just a few sessions at the keyboard. Even though we use words every day, it takes some practice to learn to push them around in a meaningful way.

Learning to push around words is equivalent, I think, to pushing around the muse, and this is something you can also get used to. Few of us have the leisure or freedom to sit down and write when the mood is upon us. If we wait for such rare opportunities, we are not likely to accomplish much writing. It is much more useful to schedule—and keep—an appointment with the muse and to learn how to conjure her presence. Do not put up with whining: ''I can't write unless I feel like it.'' Well, maybe. But you can lure yourself into feeling like it, just as you sometimes talk yourself out of a funk or into a good time.

Taking charge of your writing can be your most important first step after deciding you want to write a book. You will have to argue with yourself now and then. Writing is a lot of work, and sometimes your project won't seem worth the effort. And sometimes you will think you are not up to the task, that you are not worthy enough or skilled enough.

Talking to Your Reader

If you are having such conversations with yourself, it can help to think about who you are writing for and to what end. Perhaps you are writing mostly for yourself, to remember and contemplate your past. Your writing might then be very journal-like and not concerned with an audience. The writing itself is the goal and therefore does not warrant much shaping or editing.

But maybe you have a specific audience in mind: your children, or grandchildren, or the citizens of your community. Imagine them reading your book. What are they saying or thinking as they read? What questions do they have for you? Engage in a conversation with one of your readers.

When you write, it helps to keep your audience clearly in mind because consciousness of audience can alter what you say and how you say it. We all do this all the time—we use a sort of automatic pilot to adjust our vocabulary to the audience at hand. We see this easily when we talk to babies and toddlers—we talk "baby talk." We adjust our words to fit their ability to understand. We can witness it, too, when we watch teenagers talking to each other and compare their words to the ones they use to talk to adults.

Vocabulary, however, is only one aspect of written

communication. Every time we speak, our words convey a tone of voice. "Don't use that tone of voice with me." We've all heard it or said it. Most of the time our auto-pilot sets the tone, as it does with baby talk. But we can also intentionally adjust our tone—we might sweeten it if we want something from someone, or put an edge on it if we're irritated and want to make a point.

All writing has tone, whether the tone is achieved intentionally or not. Think about the tone of voice you want to use for your audience. It can be hard to assign definitions to tone, but it is still worth thinking about and worth keeping an eye on, because our tone can change with the story and the writing of the story. Sometimes when my writing is not going well, I slip into a negative tone. Maybe I am writing about something that is difficult for me, or maybe I am just tired. Still, I try to be aware of subtle shifts. They tell me I might need to rest or to take a different direction with the writing. I don't want my readers saying to themselves, "Don't use that tone of voice with me."

Vocabulary and tone of voice are complemented by a writer's style. We all have a writing style, even if we are not aware of it, just as we have a clothing style. And as with clothing, we can recognize each other by the way we wear our words. The comment, "That sounds like something he would say," indicates that we recognize a person's style of speech. As with tone, the task is not to create a style, but to recognize the one we use and to alter it for our means.

Style includes our habits with words, sentence structure and length, and use of analogy and metaphor. If

I were to describe my own style, I would say that I tend to use metaphor, analogy and colons in my writing; that my sentences are varied, sometimes short, sometimes long; and that I use personal experience to talk about universal concepts. I like to think that my vocabulary is precise but accessible, and that I invite the reader to walk alongside me, rather than to view me from a distance.

Another term frequently used to talk about writing is *voice*. "The writer has a strong voice." Voice is, for me, the combination of vocabulary, tone and style. It is akin, perhaps, to the "presence" of a person. One might say, for example, "She has a commanding presence, both on and off the page." It is an author's voice that makes us want to sit down and share a pot of tea them, or makes us think, "I wouldn't want to meet him in a dark alley." You already have a writing voice. As with style, the task is to recognize it and to make it work for you.

Reading What You've Written

Vocabulary, tone, style, voice. How does one juggle all those concepts in the air and still keep one's fingers moving on the keyboard? Fortunately, all four of these elements of writing come embedded in the words and sentences we use. As with our heartbeat and breath, they will take care of themselves most of the time.

We can, however, help set up these elements by deciding ahead of time what kind of a book we want to write. I don't mean deciding to write a memoir instead of a novel. I mean deciding what the memoir will look like. Will it have the flow and heft of a symphony, or will it be a collection of singular pieces, strung together the way songs are on a music album? Will it be arranged in parts, with smaller pieces in each part, or will it be in chapters, straight through from beginning to end? Will it be arranged by season? By year? Will each chapter be about a place or a character?

Fortunately, you do not have to answer all or any of these questions before you start writing. Instead, you can work on bits and pieces, as suggested in the experiments in the previous chapters and can see what order emerges from what you write.

However, once you have written some of your memoir, stop and see what shape it is taking. Then think about what you can do to fill in or enhance the shape. Trust the shape that occurs to you. If your experiments tend to lead from one to the next, you might have a symphonic arrangement underway. If the pieces tend to be autonomous, your book might be a collection of vignettes, a scrapbook of sorts. If all of your experiments are about places, maybe place is the larger subject of your work. Or is it people? Or holidays?

At some point, the shape of the book will emerge for you. Sit back and look at it—look at what it is becoming, not at what you thought it would be before you wrote it. Let the emerging shape guide you—tell you where to fill in, and where to cut. Don't worry about losing tidbits that you find fascinating. Almost everything you thought of along the way will find its way in somewhere, perhaps in a caption for a picture or in a later story. Just as your life happened to you in spite of your best efforts to make it go a certain way, try to let the story of your life happen on the page. Have faith in it. If you learn from your writing, so will your reader.

Experiments

*1. **Conjuring Your Memoir**.* Although in the end, the stories you tell should give your memoir its final shape, it can help to think about its shape before you start. Do you have a sense of how long it might be? Of what the printed book might look like? Is it hardbound or paper? What is on the cover? Have you thought about a title?

What do these things tell you about your book, about your intent in writing it and your hope for those who read it?

*2. **Conjuring Your Audience**.* To help your writing autopilot speak effectively to your audience, describe someone who might read your book. Where do they sit while reading it? What is the expression on their face? What thoughts would you like them to have when they are done with the book?

*3. **Who Are You Talking To?*** Sometimes we don't realize how much we alter our verbal style for our audience. To become aware of this, choose a single event and write about it in letters to three different audiences: a child age eight or so; a peer, especially someone who was also at the event you'll describe; and a much older person, preferably someone of authority, such as a cleric, a boss or law enforcement officer.

The event should be something that went awry or pushed the envelope of convention in some way. It might be a party where everyone overimbibed or the time you got a speeding ticket.

After you have written the three letters, compare them. Which was easiest and hardest to write? Did you use different words? What assumptions did you make in the second one, the one to someone who also participated in the event?

*4. **Write a Book Proposal.*** A book proposal is a one-page document that describes a book to a potential publisher. It usually tells what the book is about, why the author should be the one to write the book and why that publisher should publish it. Even if you do not anticipate seeking a publisher for your memoir, try writing a proposal for it. What is it like to think about your book that way?

*5. **What Are You Saying?*** It is hard to describe ourselves, but try to describe your own writing. Take a passage you have written—one of the letters you wrote in the third experiment would work. What can you say about your tone, style and voice? What do you think other people know about you from them?

CHAPTER EIGHT

Revising Your Manuscript

I lump writers into two categories: pickers and blurters. These categories do not refer to the writing itself, but rather to the process of writing.

I am a picker. I revise as I go, struggling with words and phrases, trying to get them right before I move to the next sentence or paragraph. I do this not because I am meticulous, but because I detest going back and finding a major flaw in a paragraph that requires the revision of the three paragraphs that follow it. So I pick. And I work out loud—speaking the words as I type, so I can feel them in my mouth and hear them in my ears. When I am done, I print out my work and go over it one more time, making small changes—a colon here, changing "a" to "the" there. But for the most part, the piece is done when I get to the end of it.

Blurters work the other way around. They pour out page after page of text, dumping into it everything they think of. They don't hone an image or polish a sentence or stay in one tense. Once they have everything down, they go back and rework the mess, shaping the figure that will emerge from their great blob of clay. They move whole paragraphs and even chapters, and toss out excess information as though it were yesterday's news.

There may be some people who work somewhere between these two extremes, but I don't know any of them. And neither way has an absolute advantage over the other, an advantage that would make one way right and the other way wrong. It only matters that you work in the way that is right for you.

The two methods do have one thing in common: Both rely on revision. Re-vision: to see again. It is a rare piece of writing that springs whole from the author's pen, and even then it usually has been submitted to the fire of extensive thought and has been refined in the recesses of the mind.

Both pickers and blurters are also subjected to a common problem that besets all writers, perhaps all artists. They must struggle to read and hear what they have written, not what they thought they wrote or meant to write, but what their audience will read.

It is a difficult task, for to read what we have written we must shut off our inside knowledge of our subject. There are a few ways to accomplish this. One is to set aside a piece you have just finished for a few days or a week. When you read it again, you are separated from the moment of creation, where the material you chose not to use was still active in the background of your mind and influenced your perception of the work.

Another method is to read your work out loud. The sound of your voice in your own ears and the motion of your lips subvert in part the undercurrent of chatter from your brain. If you read your work out loud frequently—I not only work out loud, but I read out loud, or at least move my lips, when I reread later on—you will discover that your tongue is an excellent editor. If you trip over words in the same place more than once, most likely there is a problem with the flat passage. Take a good look at it. Perhaps you have left out information or included too much.

Re-Vision

Revising your text is an intensely personal experience and one to be taken seriously. It is different from editing, where you are checking for grammar and sentence problems. It is, instead, a continued building of your story. Whether you are a picker or a blurter, you will still want to enhance your intuitive writing with some thoughtful revision.

If you are saying to yourself, "Well, I just say what I have to say—I just write it the way it comes out," you might consider rethinking your writing process. Your experiences and your thoughts are like a box full of photographs that have been saved haphazardly over the years. Until they go into albums, arranged in order, chronological or by theme, and captioned with the names of people and places, they are of little interest to an outside viewer. In a way, your memoir is your scrapbook. It will take time and energy to put your memories together in a meaningful way, but once you have done that, you will have a completed project that is worth your time and also the time of your reader.

Revision can be as simple as changing one word to another: forest to woods or sea to ocean. Maybe the second version has a different sound, or a different sense. These are choices of the heart and can, I think, be trusted. But what to do with passages that seem not to work, that don't quite capture the feeling or value of a scene or place? Here are a few ways to approach such problem areas.

Using Dialogue

Using dialogue is one of the quickest ways to bring life to a passage. A full conversation can be recorded, or bits of one can be used as illustration. When using dialogue, don't worry about quoting someone directly, unless you are quoting from a written text. It is the flavor of the dialogue that you want to add to your writing. If you think you might misrepresent someone, paraphrase them—say what they said in your own words, without quotation marks—or ask them to read what you have written and comment on it.

Changing Tense

We write in one of three tenses: past, present or future. Most of the time when we write about the past, we write in the past tense, but that is not a requirement. Sometimes writing about the past in the present tense lends energy to the writing. The events in my essay "The Animals at Home," in chapter four, occurred several years before I wrote the essay, but writing it and reading it in the present tense makes the experience feel more immediate.

Changing Point of View

We also write in one of three persons: first (I, me); second (you); and third (he, she, they, it). Usually when we write a memoir, we write in the first person, because we all understand that a memoir is about the author. However, it can help sometimes when we're stuck on a bit of writing to write in the second or third person instead of the first. I've done this many times, especially when I am writing about difficult subjects such as death or loss. It seems to free me. I can say, "She rocked herself to sleep in grief" where I was not willing to say, "I rocked myself to sleep in grief."

Once done with the writing, I am usually able to revise it into the first person, but sometimes not. I have several poems that stay in the third person, because I still do not want to claim the experience for myself.

The memoir is written from the author's point of view—it is the author's story. But parts of a memoir can also be written from another person's point of view. For instance, I wrote a story once about getting lost when I was about four years old. I wrote in the past tense, about the little girl I was. Then I wrote the same story from my mother's point of view. Although both pieces are about one event, the stories are dramatically different.

Writing from someone else's point of view, even if you don't use the passage in your memoir, can help you think of things to say that you might not come to from your own point of view.

Looking for Chinks

Often when we write, we get tired and skimp on information. Or perhaps we are on a roll with a subject and do not want to slow down to add detail. I can tell when I do this because I start using parentheses. "We went down to the ocean early in the morning (we put the picnic basket on the sand) and stood knee-deep in salt water, watching the sun come up." My first inclination, when I reread the sentence, is to just omit the parentheses and its contents, but usually that is a mistake. I probably thought of the detail for a reason. My task is not to eliminate it, but to treat it as a chink in the story—a little space where I might add some interesting detail.

First, however, I have to get it out of the way of the other sentence, which wants to flow forward without interruption. Then I can consider the picnic basket, and perhaps give it a paragraph of its own: "Later in the morning, when the sun splashed relentlessly over the sea, we took our picnic basket from the car and sought shade under palm trees that stood back from the water. The basket held only bare necessities: food and drink. Stripped by the sun, the sand, the salt and the water of greater requirements of body and soul, it contained all we needed."

Never mind that we had brought the basket out of the car to begin with. The story tells better this way, and my task is not to report what happened so much as to re-create the spirit of what happened.

Trimming Dross

While there are often places in our writing where we can expand, there are certainly as many where we can cut. I almost started this paragraph with a comment on the word "dross," but when I looked at what I'd written, I realized that the definition did not forward the task of the paragraph, which is to talk about editing out dross, not defining the word itself.

Dross—that which is worthless or trivial—is not easy to find in our writing. I personally am enamored of every word I write, and I hate to give up any one of them. Therefore, to keep my writing clean, I keep a second file open on my computer screen and move excess words and passages into it. I save it under "Notes" for that chapter, and I am often pleased that later I find captions for pictures there or tidbits that fit in a later chapter. The second file reminds me of my mother's sewing basket, where she kept buttons she could use for mending clothes. While all of the buttons were perfectly good, clearly they had to be matched carefully with appropriate garments.

In the end, you are the one who decides if information moves your story forward or bogs it down. You'll come to understand this with practice.

Using a Dictionary

One of the best things you can do for your writing is to look up words in the dictionary, not only words you don't know, but words you do know. Words are your paints, your clay. When you look them up, check their etymologies—their origins—and look at the words above and below them. Wonder about them. Hold them in awe. You will come to understand in a new way their qualities and properties, and your understanding will bring a nice glow to your writing.

Using a Thesaurus

Thesaurus is a Greek word, meaning "treasury," and a treasury is a place where we keep that which is valuable to us, in this case, a collection of words, the most treasured possession of a writer.

A thesaurus is different from that other collection of words, the dictionary. Instead of definitions, it presents synonyms for words. "Color: hue, tone, tint," each entry a treasure within a treasure, the words rubbing against each other with the pleasure of familiarity.

Many writers like to keep a thesaurus handy for those inevitable moments when the brain goes dead, or when fresh words escape us, or when we have used one certain word too many times and want an alternative. The flood of options in the listings not only offers substitutes, but often inspires thought about the words themselves or about what we have been writing.

Still, I take a cautious approach to looking for words in a book rather than in my head. I believe the words we use spontaneously carry with them sounds and feelings that are attached to our thoughts and to the writing that we have just committed to the page. Words picked from a list might not have those associations, even if their meanings are correct. If you are feeling stuck or want to search for a word you think is missing from your writing, consider using a dictionary in addition to or instead of a thesaurus. In addition to the definition of the word you are looking up, look at the words above and below it, and look at its etymology. These are treasures in themselves and might lead you to other treasures you had not thought of.

Listening to Your Readers

It is hard to be critical of your own writing, which you worked so hard to make right. It is harder still for most of us to listen to what someone else has to say about it.

Still, unless you bury your work in a box and hide it under the bed, that day will come for you.

Most professional writers have "readers"—editors or friends whom we trust with our work, trust to tell us something useful about what we've written. Before you search for your readers, it is important to know what you want from them. If you have not done a lot of writing, you will probably want to know if your work is "good." If your readers are not also writers, that's what they will want to tell you: "This is good."

But a judgment of good or bad is not of much use to you, for we all have different definitions of good, and readers who are not also writers will usually not feel adequate to give you practical feedback. They can, however, let you know about their experience of reading your work.

It is therefore up to you to guide your readers in their responses. Tell them that you don't want to know if the work is good or bad. You want to know what it was like for them to read it. Did they feel any emotions? Was there a story they especially liked? Was there a place where they got confused? They will still want to say to you, "This is good," so you will have to help them get beyond that. "Why is it good? Can you say?" And they will try, usually successfully, to tell you what they felt while they read.

The second part of receiving feedback on your writing is deciding how to use it. Remember that you know more about your work than anyone, and in the end you are the one who knows if it is "right." As you progress with your book and get used to hearing feedback, you will develop a method of using—or ignoring—the responses of others.

One way to practice using "constructive criticism"—I prefer the term *feedback*—is to join or form a writers' group. There might be two of you or five or six. I think six is a good top limit; it provides a variety of responses but keeps the discussion intimate. The members of the group might write in many genres: fiction, poetry, memoir, nonfiction. That does not matter. What matters are the ground rules for the group. Here are mine:

1. Members always get a hard copy of the work under discussion. These can be passed out at the meeting. Reading and responding under pressure sharpens one's reading abilities.

2. Works under discussion are read out loud before the discussion, again at the end of the discussion and sometimes during the discussion. The author can read first, but it is a good idea for someone else to read subsequent times.

3. No judgments are made. If someone says, "This is good," they can be prompted to say why. Appropriate responses are, "I felt like I was walking along with you because of the little details you give about the path," or "I got lost here—you are in the doorway, and then you are in the car—I don't know how you got there."

4. The discussion includes comments on the writer's style to reveal techniques, vocabulary and grammar common to the writer: "I notice you use a lot of short sentences." "There are many scientific words in this piece, where in the one you wrote last week the vocabulary was

more casual." "You use colors a lot in your writing—and circles—there are so many round things here—they give me a sense of completion and fullness."

Entitlement

As your memoir develops, you will begin to know intuitively when you are done with parts of it and when you are done with the whole. You can get feedback on this from others, but in the end, you must decide. Give yourself time away from the work, so you can read it the way your audience will. And read the whole thing out loud, so you can hear what you said.

When you are done with the manuscript, you will need a title for it. You might have come across one along the way or even had one from the beginning. If you had one from the beginning, make sure it is the title for the memoir you wrote, not the one you intended to write.

If you are stuck for a title, you can try several things. First, write in a few words what your book is about: "Summers at Aunt Marion's house." Aha! A good subtitle. Now, what is the first image that comes to your mind when you think about Aunt Marion's house? "Blue pond, green meadow." You have a possible title: *Blue Pond, Green Meadow: Summers With Aunt Marion*.

Think about secondary meanings to your title: What might a blue pond stand for? A green meadow? Are those meanings compatible with your story? If so, good. If not, look for other images that better tell your readers what they are getting into when they read your book.

Experiments

1. Past to Present. Take one of your experiments from earlier chapters and notice what tense you wrote it in. If it is in the past tense, rewrite it in the present, or vice versa. You might have to change some details. Notice what they are and what the changes mean to your reader.

2. Me to Thee. Take one of your earlier writings and write it in a different person—instead of saying, "I did this," say, "She or he did this." Notice how the changes affect the detail you give and the tone of the writing.

3. Point of View. Using one of the experiments from an earlier chapter, write about an event from the point of view of a person other than yourself. How does this change the information you present? What new understanding of the event do you gain from looking at it from another point of view?

4. Chinks. When you are revising a passage from your memoir, look for places where you might open up the text and insert new information—a place where you can expand a description or include a new character.

5. Rigorous Revising. This is one of my favorite experiences. Take any piece you have written and cut the number of words by about half. Do not expect the piece to be the same when you are done with it. You may have a very simple story instead of a complex one. It may have one character instead of many. Look at the two pieces and compare them. Sometimes the shorter one is more intense and direct, sometimes it feels incomplete.

Revise in any way you want—delete whole paragraphs or just words here and there. Adjust the content as you need to so the story still makes sense. When you are done, you can reexpand the piece—but try to do it without looking at the original. Instead, look for chinks where you can build the story anew.

CHAPTER NINE

Editing your Manuscript

Editing and revising are not the same thing. Revision of a manuscript is carried out by the author and alters the content of a piece. Editing is carried out by the author or an editor and is, technically, the preparation of a manuscript for publication or presentation. If you are lucky, somewhere along the road you will find a good "blue pencil" person to edit your memoir. In the book industry, editors use blue pencil lead to mark up the typeset pages of a manuscript because the blue color is not picked up on the photographic plates from which books are printed.

You want an editor who will come to your manuscript with a fresh eye, who will catch odd little problems that you will not see. But you are also the editor of your work. Being attuned to grammar, spelling, punctuation and other formalities helps you stay attuned to the writing itself. A sentence gone awry is often an indication that the thinking has also gone awry, and it is your job to see that.

Most of us don't completely understand the conventions of writing that we use every day—the possessive apostrophe, for example, or the semicolon, and for the most part, we don't need to. But as writers, we must care about these things. The conventions of writing help keep our writing clear and move the reader along without pause. The rest of this chapter reviews some of the more common conventions that cause problems for writers and readers. For other forms, refer to a composition handbook—every textbook publisher offers one, and your public library probably has several. You can browse through it in short order and will quickly understand conventions that have always been a mystery to you.

Transitions

The word *transition* comes from the same root as *transportation* and *transfer*. In writing, a transition carries the reader from one idea to another. It is used most often at the beginning of paragraphs—almost every paragraph. It says to the reader, "I was talking about that, but now I'm talking about this." Here is an example.

Paragraph one:

"In winter, there is a lot of snow, and the weather is very cold."

Paragraph two:

"While it is cold in winter, in spring the temps begin to rise."

"While it is cold in winter" is a transition. It summarizes the previous paragraph and introduces the next one.

To better understand transitions between paragraphs, spend some time browsing through articles in popular magazines. Read the first phrase of every paragraph. This will help you to recognize transitions and to understand their value.

You can also hear transitions on television news programs. Listen for them during the switch from the news segment to the weather. "Well, Dan, it may have been sizzling in Congress today, but we're plenty cool here in the Delta."

In my example paragraphs, the transitions are: "to better understand transitions between paragraphs" and the word "also" in "You can also hear."

Transitions are not required for every paragraph, but if your writing feels choppy or your readers say they get lost, transitions can help fill in blanks and maintain flow.

Introductory Phrase Punctuation

An introductory phrase is a set of words that leads into a sentence. In a previous paragraph, I said, "In writing, a transition carries the reader from one idea to another." You might note that I put a comma after "in writing." This comma after an introductory phrase is optional, but I recommend using it. It can keep the grammar of a sentence clear. If I do not use it in my example, the reader starts the sentence thinking it says "In writing a transition . . ." By placing the comma after the intro phrase, I keep the information straight: "In writing, a transition carries . . ."

I also recommend using the comma after a long introductory phrase to keep the syntax—the organization of the sentence—clear for the reader.

"Although the sun was out and the snow was melting off the roof I did not go to town."

"Although the sun was out and the snow was melting off the roof, I did not go to town."

"I did not go to town" is the main part of the sentence. The comma, though optional, helps the readers know when they get to the point of the sentence.

The Possessive Apostrophe

The possessive apostrophe shows possession, ownership: "The cat's tail" means the tail belongs to the cat. That part is simple. Where most of us get confused is when there is more than one cat and more than one tail. That is because the possessive apostrophe is used with the letter *s* which is also used to show plurals. Here's a little rundown that might help clear it up for you.

If the noun is singular and has an *s* at the end, the *s* must be there to show possession. It therefore requires a possessive apostrophe, which goes before the *s*: "The cat's tail."

If the noun is plural, it already has an *s* so the apostrophe goes after: "The cats' tails." If we said "the cats' tail," it would mean several cats shared one tail.

Now, exceptions to the rule. What about a car owned by Susan and Bill? *Bill and Susan's car*—one possessive apostrophe for one car. But if they own separate cars, then it is *Bill's and Susan's cars.*

And, with nouns that are plural by definition, such as *women, men* and *children,* the apostrophe always comes before the *s.* The *s* cannot mean the word is plural, as it is plural by definition, hence the *s* must be possessive: *women's, men's, children's.* This is correct in spite of what you see on restroom doors and sports' scoreboards (mens basketball should be men's).

A last category of words further complicates matters: possessive pronouns are possessive by definition. *Theirs* means "it belongs to them." No possessive apostrophe is required. This is also true for *its, yours, hers* and *ours,* as for *mine* and *his.*

The pronoun *its* offers special confusion because of the contraction *it's* which means "it is." If you have trouble with this, the solution is simple. When you are proofreading your paper, if you come across *it's,* read it as "it is." You'll know immediately if you used the right form.

Soundalike Words

There; their; they're; theirs; there's. If you get these words mixed up, stop and think them through when you proofread.

There includes here—"here and there."

Their includes I—indicating person—"it is their way."

They're—"they are."

Theirs means "belongs to them."

There's means "there is."

Theirs' and *their's* are not words—possessive pronouns do not require a possessive apostrophe.

Other Common Word Errors

A lot is two words. Some day it will probably be one, but for now it is two.

Affect and effect. *Affect* is a verb: "It will affect us." *Effect* is a noun, and the consequence of the verb: "The effect was devastating." I think of them as working in alphabetical order—first the action (it affects) then the end (the effect). *Affect* is also a noun, in psychology circles; it means "emotion."

There's means "there is." It is commonly used today in place of *there are.* "There's a lot of trees down from the storm." By the end of this century, it will be accepted as correct, but for now it's wrong.

Gender Sensitivity

Language is ever changing, and to those who say we should not make new words or use old words in new ways, I say, "Doest thou so thinketh?"

The most exciting word change of our times is the use of *their* as a singular possessive pronoun. Traditionally, it is a plural possessive pronoun. "The students left their books out in the rain." Now we are likely to hear someone also say, "The student left their book out in the rain." One student . . . their book.

This new use of the pronoun *their* evolved spontaneously from a culture that struggled for several decades to solve the problem of gender sensitivity in its singular pronouns—his and her. "The student left his/her book in the rain." Using *their* is an ingenuous adaptation, and it is here to stay, although the grammar books won't say so for at least several more decades. You might consider who your audience is when deciding issues of gender. A long-established press will likely adhere to traditional rules of grammar, but your friends and family may prefer a more conversational tone in your writing. You have probably used it yourself, and if you watch for it, you will see it in advertising and hear it on both the local and national news. You have also read it in this book.

They and *them* are also sometimes used as a singular pronouns but have not achieved the common status of *their.*

Gender Equity

Language is powerful and it matters how we use it. The use of the noun *man* to mean "man and woman" is rapidly fading, as it should. Our now-fading acceptance of the convention is grounded in English common law that states the man and the woman are one, and the one is the man.

As noted earlier, as a society, we have found a way to resolve the problem of the gender sensitive pronoun, but many writers are still challenged when they try to keep their writing both fresh and gender-free. The first approach to a problem sentence is to make the subject plural: "He controls the car by keeping the wheel loose in his hands" can sometimes become "They control the car by keeping the wheel loose in their hands." But sometimes that just doesn't work, and sometimes "their" as a singular pronoun still doesn't sound right to us.

When that happens, try changing the subject of the sentence: "The car is controlled by keeping the wheel loose in the hands."

Or, try rearranging the sentence in a larger way: "A computer operator types for hours on end, and unless she keeps her wrists straight and her shoulders back, she will experience shooting pains from her elbows down to her fingers.''

"When typing for hours on end, a computer operator can prevent shooting pains from elbow to wrist by keeping the wrists and shoulders straight.''

Writing Out Numbers

Single digit numbers, one through nine, should be written out. Double-digit numbers may be written out or presented as digits. Dates are always expressed in digits. More information on rules of style is available in style guides, and libraries usually carry several guides, including *The Chicago Manual of Style* and *The Associated Press Stylebook and Libel Manual.*

Giving Credit

Even in a memoir, you may sometimes find yourself using material that belongs to someone else. If so, you should give credit by adding a simple citation into the text. Footnotes are used today only in scholarly publications, and even there they usually give way to a simpler form of citation. If you want to quote a passage from a magazine, weave the title into your paragraph, and include dates and other information in parentheses at the end of the paragraph. "In an essay published in *Summer Weekly,* John Smith, a local horticulturist, said that our country was the best one for growing roses (August 1977, page 22).''

A similar format can be used for citing books and other resources, including movies and Internet sources. If you will use a lot of such citations, you should go to the library and find an MLA style guide. Developed by the Modern Language Association of America, it covers proper citation techniques for literary publications. Scientific publications use the APA style guide (American Psychological Association).

If you interviewed someone, you might also want to include credit, but the information can be given informally in the text. "Esmeralda and I talked one sunny day in the summer of 1983."

Formatting Dialogue

There are a few rules for presenting dialogue in writing. Phrases placed in quotation marks should be direct quotations—they should be exactly what was said. If the conversation is not directly quoted, you can omit the marks.

Mary said, "I never did like her." (These should be Mary's exact words.)

Mary said she never did like her. (This is a paraphrase of what Mary said—a reporting of the gist of her comments.)

A quote within a quote uses single apostrophes, while the larger quote uses double: "She said, 'I never said that.' "

When writing an extended dialogue, you can use a new paragraph every time the speaker shifts, even if the paragraphs are very short.

"Well, enough of that," said Sam.

Susan said, "I agree."

Note that the quoted material is set off with a

comma, whether it comes before or after acknowledgment of the speaker.

Punctuation

Most of us use punctuation intuitively, and that serves us well enough. If you want to know the finest of points, refer to *The Chicago Manual of Style*, which should be available in your public library. Here are a few niceties to be aware of.

Commas and periods always go inside quotation marks.

She said, "It's true."

"That's right," she said.

Question and exclamation marks might go inside or outside quotation marks, depending on the sense of the sentence. If the quotation is a question or exclamation, the mark goes inside; if not, it goes outside.

Did she say, "I'm not going"?

She said, "Should I go?"

Semicolons and colons are placed outside of quotation marks.

"Let's go"; and they did.

She did not like the song "Summer Blues": It made her sad.

A colon indicates that the information after it is an expansion or example of the information before it. The part before the colon must be a complete sentence, but the part after can be complete or a phrase.

She went to the store for fruit: bananas, apples, oranges.

A semicolon is a variation on a period and carries

the same rules as a period: The information before and after must be complete sentences. The semicolon is used to indicate a strong relationship between two thoughts.

Love is the strangest of human emotions; it causes both pain and joy.

A colon would also be appropriate in this example sentence.

When using parentheses, the period goes inside the closing parenthesis unless the whole sentence is enclosed. For example, "(the period goes outside this parenthesis)." "(But inside this one.)"

If you are uncertain about the proper punctuation of a sentence, you can try using dashes—they are an informal way to show relationship between ideas in a sentence.

Experiments

1. Playing With Sentences. Even the greatest musicians practice playing scales on their instruments, and vocalists practice singing notes. As a writer, you might want to hone your writing skills. One way to do this is to play with sentences you wrote spontaneously.

Try taking a sentence from something you have already written and revise it in at least two different ways. Make verbs into nouns, nouns into verbs. Meld two sentences into one, separate one into two. Use a semicolon.

Read all versions of your sentence and notice how

change in the order of the words changes the sense or meaning of the sentence.

2. Playing With Paragraphs. We tend to organize our paragraphs spontaneously when we write, but that doesn't mean we have to leave them that way. Try re-arranging a paragraph you've written. Put the last sentence first, and vice versa. What happens to the sense of things?

Check your paragraph against the ones that precede and follow it. Do you use transitions to keep your reader on track?

3. Language Sensitivity. Take out one of your experiments from earlier chapters, and look at it the way you might look at a picture to see what it is made of. Do you use commas after introductory phrases? Do you use *he, him* and *his* as general pronouns? If so, try re-arranging your sentences to make them gender-free, if that's appropriate to the context of the sentence.

4. Punctuating Your Punctuation. Look at something you've written and notice the kind of punctuation you use. If you never use colons, semicolons or dashes, you might want to consider them. They add variety to your writing, and they may help you think of new ways to present your thoughts.

CHAPTER TEN

Helping Others Write Their Stories

Writing is usually a solitary task. Ideas for a story or book come to us in the privacy of our minds, and the writing itself is done in what some might call a terrible solitude: We are faced with only our selves and the blank screen or paper, and it screams to us not in invitation but almost with scorn.

Well, that is often how I feel when I get down to writing. I understand, therefore, why those who do not have some internal drive to write down their lives cannot easily be talked into it. A strong desire to write—to do the writing itself—is probably a prerequisite for any major writing project.

Still, for writers, it is hard to let go of a story that begs to be told but is not ours to tell. If we feel strongly about it, we might take it on as ours to tell. Such a drastic measure, however, is not usually necessary. Through mentorship and collaboration, it is often possible to bring to the page the story of a reluctant teller. The techniques can also be used in working with children and young adults, and in writing collaborative or collective memoirs.

Helping Children Write Their Stories
It is not difficult to get children to tell their stories. They understand, better than adults, that all of life is a

story. If you want a child age eleven or up to consider writing a memoir, you can first set up a format for them, so they can move from scene to scene without having to understand the overall picture.

You might begin by making a list of subjects, such as birthdays, holidays, summer vacations or favorite relatives. Most of the experiments in chapters two through four should also work. Then ask the child to write about them. If they have trouble getting started, suggest that they begin with, "I remember when. . . ." If that doesn't help, suggest that they write the story as a letter. "Dear Grandma—last week we all went to the beach for a picnic. . . ."

The writings from a child are not likely to flow together in a continuous narrative, but they can be put together as a series of vignettes. They can also be used as sidebars in your own memoir. A sidebar is a bit of writing set aside from the main text, usually in a box. It serves as an illustration of sorts. Examples of sidebars can be seen in popular magazines where they are used to present tips or step-by-step instructions.

A child's writings can also be published in a home-made pamphlet. This is easy to do today using a home computer or the services of a photocopy shop. You might suggest to the children in a family or in a neighborhood that they each write their recollection of a single event they all participated in—a holiday, or a picnic, or a vacation. Each version will be wonderfully different, and they can all be brought together in one publication. Even the story of a child too young to write can be recorded by another child and included in the publication.

If the child you are working with has no interest in writing, you can interview them, the same as you would an adult. When you have written your version of the interview, you can show it to them. They might want to add something or take something away. They might even want to take it over and make it their own by revising and adding to it.

Although you might not have a grand scheme for using children's memoirs, you can keep them in mind when traveling, visiting or for occasions when children get bored. Boredom can be a trigger for contemplation. With a new notebook to write in and some specific writing prompts—such as, "Do you remember your last birthday?"—a child can learn the pleasures of claiming time for oneself and, at the same time, claiming one's stories.

Helping Adolescents Write Their Stories

Adolescents are more likely than children to understand the larger narrative of the memoir, but they still might need help getting started. The experiments in chapters two through five should work for them. If they are mildly interested in such a project but seem unwilling to start, remember they face the same blank page you do when you try to start writing. You can help them by suggesting an organization—write a few paragraphs by year, going backward in time as far as you can remember, or write about your birthday, going back as many years as you can, even skipping years if that helps.

Or, suggest that they write about places they lived or people who have been important to them.

The writings of adolescents are more likely to take the form of a journal or diary, forms that have the self as audience. You need not be bothered by this. The act of writing can be valuable in itself, especially when we are in transition, as teenagers are. And some day the stories may serve as the basis for a memoir that includes a consciousness of audience.

As with children, if you want stories from young adults who have no interest in writing, ask if you can just talk about their past, their memories, and if you can use them in your book or for a family anthology. Be sure to show them what you've written, so they can contribute more if they want.

Helping Older Adults Write Their Stories

"Grandma! You should write that down!" "It wasn't anything," Grandma replies. "We all did it."

Many of us love to hear stories about the old days. They help us understand the older people in our lives, and they help us understand who we are and where we came from. But our interest is often not shared by the people who have the stories.

If you want someone's story recorded, and they are willing to do the writing, you can help them by providing prompts and structure. You can ask them to write about a given year or a sequence of events: "What did you do after high school?" Tell them not to worry about the book as a whole—that you'll take care of that by putting together the pieces they write.

If the reluctant storyteller has trouble getting started, try engaging in correspondence. You can write and ask questions, and they can write back with answers. This also allows for discussion—you can ask for more information or clarification.

With the consent of the storyteller, you can then weave the writing into a memoir, or use it to illustrate or enhance your own project. Always, of course, ask for permission to do this, and ask for feedback on the way you organize the writing and on what you say about it.

If the storyteller is just not interested in writing the story, you can ask if they would be willing to collaborate with you. They tell the story out loud, and you write it down and shape it. The book can be presented in several ways. It can be under the storyteller's name, "as told to" you. Or it can be presented as a collaboration: "by Sally Sally, with Jane Jane." Or you can "ghost write" it—be invisible, except in the acknowledgments.

You can, of course, also co-opt the story—take it for your own, with the consent of the storyteller. You can acknowledge the source of the story in your book's title subtitle—*Blue Pond, Green Meadow: The Story of Sally Sally* by Jane Jane.

Whether you or the storyteller is doing the writing, the techniques and experiments in chapters two through five can be useful in getting the story underway.

Writing Someone Else's Story

If you write someone else's story, it is not technically a memoir. However, the lines between genres are constantly being nudged. We now have fictional memoirs and historical novels. In the end, you can write a story the way you want. Remember if you are writing someone else's story, you should try at least occasionally to look at it from that person's point of view. What approach would you want someone to take who is writing about your life? Are you satisfied with the way you are thinking about and presenting your subject?

If you proceed with the writing, the techniques recommended in this book should help you write successfully about someone else's life. Concrete, sensory details about events, objects, people and places can bring life to the story. Interviews and research can offer you perceptions and perspectives that you might not come to on your own.

As you move along with your writing, imagine your subject reading your book. I do not say that so you will say only nice things. A book that says only nice things is called a hagiography, and in the end is usually not believable. I say it so you will think about the consequences of your writing, for yourself and for your subject. The truth as you see it may be harsh, but if it is the truth, then writing it may be worth the consequences. Be careful, however, not to confuse truth with revenge. If you are uncertain about what you've written, ask someone you trust to read it and comment. In the end, though, the decision and the consequences are yours.

Collaborating on a Memoir

If you are writing a memoir about a place or an experience you shared with someone, you might want to work on it together. This can be fascinating and fun, and it can be frustrating and even infuriating.

If you are going to collaborate on a memoir or any writing, be sure to start out by writing down—not just discussing—how the collaboration will proceed and who will do what. In the writing, little details will get straightened out and assumptions, which can cause grief, have a good chance of being revealed.

At the same time, you should discuss, and write down, how you expect the memoir to look when it is done and what you will do with it. Will you self-publish it? Will both of you seek a publisher, or just one of you? How will you split expenses and proceeds? What if one person ends up writing more than the other?

As with businesses, more than one collaboration has resulted in the loss of friendship. Try to preempt this by agreeing ahead of time that the first time one of you feels uncomfortable about something, you will bring it up and discuss it. Agree that you will both treat it as a business matter to resolve and will try not to be hurt by the problem. This is not easy to do, but it is important. If you don't feel you can have that kind of relationship with another person, I recommend that you write on your own.

In the end, you might both decide to pursue the writing project separately, and that can work just fine, even if you are writing about the same thing. Everyone's story is different, even if it's the same story, and everyone tells their story differently. You don't have to worry about the other person telling "your" story—no one can tell it the way you will. You also don't need to worry about there being more than one book on a similar topic. It is an indication of interest in the subject, and many people will want to read one book because they've read the other.

If you do decide to collaborate on a book, consult the next chapter on publishing when you are ready to go to press, if not before. You should have a contract that specifies who gets what under what circumstances. You might trust each other and work well together, but if one of you dies, the other will be dealing with an heir who might not see things the way the authors did.

Coordinating a Collective Memoir

In the last decade, there has been a great deal of interest in genealogy research, and in the history of places and specific time periods. This is inspired in part by the maturing of the baby boomer crowd and in part by our passage into the new millennium. Local histories are also inspired by anniversaries—many communities are marking centennial or bicentennial anniversaries.

Family and neighborhood memoirs can be wonderfully satisfying to work on, and with the explosion of the Internet, coordination and cooperation have become easy. If you are interested in such a project, you can edit it yourself or you can seek collaborators, coeditors, who will help you with the work.

There are advantages and disadvantages to both methods. If you work on your own, most of the tasks will fall to you, but you will also have the authority—author-ity—to make editorial and production decisions on your own. If you have a strong vision of how you'd like the project to go and what you'd like it to become, do not hesitate to claim this right for yourself. It is your idea, and you will bear its expenses, consequences and benefits. You will be the editor, and your editorial voice will guide and shape the content of the work. This does not mean you have to work absolutely alone. You will be asking for writing contributions, and you can ask for help with other tasks in exchange for credit in the book and discounted copies. Just be clear for yourself that you are the editor and that the final choices are yours.

To determine if you have a strong vision for the project, write down your ideas about it. What would the book look like? Who would read it? What understandings would they acquire from the reading? How would you decide what goes into it? Try to determine how strongly you feel about the outcome of the project. Let yourself feel ownership for it. When envisioning a project that includes work by others, it is tempting to let others also take on some of the authority for the project. If you do not have a strong vision, that might be all right, but if the idea is yours and you have a sense of how you want the book to be, avoid giving up your editorial position.

Group Efforts

If you do not have a strong vision for the project but only an idea of it, and you do not want to shoulder the major responsibility for its completion, you might want to gather together an editorial board. This board will create the vision for the project and work collectively to make it come about. If you do this, be prepared to yield to the vision of the group, which might be different from your original vision. Early on, at a meeting, talk about the outcome of the work—who will hold legal rights to the document and how profits, if there are any, will be handled. If the board is unwilling to understand or discuss these issues, reconsider working on your own.

If a family or neighborhood memoir is going to be created by an editorial board, it is also important to understand the making of decisions by consensus. Consensus means everyone agrees to go along with a point, even if some disagree with it. For consensus to work, the goals and vision of the project need to be clear, and individuals need to understand the value of decision-making by consensus. If you get to a point where your only way out seems to be to call for a vote, then your work is not done. You need to talk more, to look again at the goals of the project and to help individuals find a place for their goals within the larger context.

If the formation and functioning of an editorial board seems like a project in itself, it is. But taking care of board business at the beginning of a project can be the salvation of the project in the end. It can help to write a brief, one-sentence mission statement for the board and to refer to it frequently when you get stuck in discussions. A mission statement can be as simple as, "Using the many voices of its citizens, we intend to tell the story of the origins of the neighborhood known as Richfield." Rereading the statement out loud can help everyone remember the inspiration for the project.

Once you have decided to go forward with a collective memoir, either on your own or as a group, you will want to issue a call for submissions. This one-page flyer states the purpose of the publication, asks for submissions and states what contributors will receive in return, usually one or two copies of the book and a discount on the purchase of additional copies. In the flyer you can ask for essays, letters, stories, printable memorabilia, photographs and any other forms that interest you. State a deadline for submissions that allows at least six months for putting together the book before it goes to press.

The work you did in establishing your board or setting your personal editorial goals will be paid off in full when the submissions start coming in. Your original inspiration will be bolstered by the passion of the stories, and the larger story of your family or neighborhood will begin to emerge. Giving birth to it, in the form of a collective memoir, can be a happy, satisfying and worthwhile experience.

Creating an Online Memoir

The World Wide Web offers new opportunities for researching and creating personal or collective memoirs. You can present your project on a Web site that can be visited by family, friends and neighbors. There they can find out what you are writing about and what you are looking for. You can set up an e-mail link so they can write to you with their versions of the places, people and events you want to know more about. You can post questions that they can answer. "I know Aunt Maude was related to us on our father's side, but does anyone know more than that?" "There is a homemade bench at the bus stop at Seventy-third and Lyndale—does anyone know where it came from?" You can post responses to the questions so others can read and respond to them.

The e-mail link you set up can be a private one that goes only to you. But you can also set up a group discussion using an electronic bulletin board or a list-serv. An electronic bulletin board is housed on a Web site. When you post a message on a bulletin board, everyone who visits the site can read the message. They can also post their responses to it on the board. The entire discussion can then be read as it evolves.

A list-serv, rather than existing on a Web site, is maintained through e-mail. Someone sets up a list to which people can subscribe. When a message is sent to the list, it goes to all subscribers. When a subscriber replies to a message, the reply also goes to everyone. The list-serv is different from the bulletin board in that only the message or the reply of the moment goes out to the list. The board carries the cumulative messages and responses.

You can also create a group e-mail list using any e-mail program. You put the addresses of the people you want to contact under a group name. You might use the group name "Memoir" for those conversing about the project. When you send an e-mail to "Memoir," it goes to everyone listed in the group. If someone replies to your message, however, the reply goes only to you.

There is a caveat to be aware of when you use electronic correspondence, whether it is e-mail or a bulletin board. Remember that it is easy to copy or forward an electronic message: Someone you do not know, or do know, may read your words. And messages are usually stored in the electricity of a server for unlimited time. If you have something to say that you don't want certain people to read, save it for a face-to-face conversation.

Besides using the Internet to research and gather stories for your personal or collective memoir, you can also use it to publish the work. You can create a Web site where anyone can read the memoir free of charge, or you can set it up so people have to pay a fee to download it to their computers, where they can then read it. See chapter eleven for information on copyright protection of online publications.

If you do not understand Web sites, or you understand them but don't know how to create them, get someone to help you. There is almost certainly someone in the family or neighborhood who can explain them to you, and can even create and maintain sophisticated Web sites. You can also learn about them through community education classes.

Experiments

1. Memoirs by Children. You do not have to be an adult to write a memoir; children can write them, too. Explain to them that the word *memoir* comes from the word *memory*, and ask them what they remember about a specific time: "Do you remember when your cousins visited here last summer?'' Then ask them to write down what they remember. If the children are young, they will naturally record concrete, sensory details: ''Abigail brought her doll, and we played with it under the tree.'' If they are older, they might turn to abstractions: ''We had fun.'' If they are writing in abstractions, ask them to provide examples and details. Have them close their eyes and picture a scene, then write down everything they can remember.

2. *Memoirs by Adolescents.* Adolescents are especially prone to writing in abstractions. They ''feel terrible'' or ''love this'' or ''hate that.'' Perhaps this is because they are beginning to evaluate their lives—which is, of course, a good thing. If they are willing to work on a memoir, it can help to show them how to use concrete, sensory details about their feelings. Ask them if their feelings have color or texture. They might be surprised to discover their joy is red, their sadness is blue. Ask them also to try listing examples of abstract thoughts and feelings: Being at the beach is an example of joy, for example. The experiments in chapters three and four might be especially useful to an adolescent who is writing a memoir.

3. *Memoirs by Older Adults.* Older adults who want to write a memoir will usually do so on their own. If they want some guidance, they could use the ideas and information in this book to get them going. The only problem some older adults have is that the inspiration for writing a memoir does not come from them, but from someone else—someone who wants the older person's life passage recorded.

If you know someone who has a life story that you think needs to be told, but the person is not interested in the process, consider collaborating on a memoir. The person talks; you write. The person reflects; you shape words into sentences, sentences into paragraphs, paragraphs into chapters. The experiments in this book can serve as discussion prompts.

To get started, and to see if the process will work for the two of you, try working together on a single story from a single period of time. It might be about holiday traditions or how birthdays were celebrated. Then, to get a feel for how a full memoir might look, you can print the story in a little pamphlet and send it to family and friends. The responses you get might help you decide how to proceed with a larger project.

4. Creating a Family or Neighborhood Memoir. A memoir does not have to be a full-blown book. It can be a pamphlet, printed from a home computer. If your family or neighborhood is having a reunion or some other ritual gathering, you can fly a trial collective memoir. Ask everyone to send in a story about a specific topic: children's summer games, winter skating rinks, Sunday school. Collect the writings into a pamphlet and print enough for everyone. Distribute the pamphlets at the family or neighborhood event. If the reaction is positive, you might be able to form an editorial board on the spot that could work on a larger project for the next year's event.

5. Browsing the Web for Memoirs. As you work on a memoir, you can use the Web in at least two ways. (1) You can search for information on your subject, and

(2) you can see how other people use the Web to present or publish their memoirs, whether personal or collective.

Spend some time browsing the Web using "memoir" as a search term. Also search for the names of people or places you are interested in. You might be very surprised by what you turn up.

CHAPTER ELEVEN

Publishing your Memoir

Publication is the presentation of a written work to an audience. The document itself might be photocopied and stapled at the spine or printed professionally on fine paper with a hard cover. In effect, both methods, and all those in between, are the frame for your painting, the performance of your song.

Even if you intend for your memoir to be read only by a few family members, I urge you to publish it—to present it in book-fashion for your readers. If you feel your story exceeds the bounds of the family, you might also seek publication of it by a literary or commercial publisher. The story of the least life, written eloquently and with insight, can be of interest to a public at large. Witness the success of *Angela's Ashes* by Frank McCourt. A story of his growing up in poverty in Ireland, it is a best-seller not because of the facts of the story, but because of McCourt's writing style and voice.

A Little Publishing Glossary

Advance: Royalties paid to an author prior to the publication of a book. Also called "advance against royalties," the publisher recoups the advance from first profits from the book. When the advance is paid back, the author receives additional royalties from sales.

Back list: Books published in previous seasons or years.

Broadside: A single sheet of paper, printed on one side

and often illustrated. Broadsides are most often used for publishing poetry. They may be any size and are usually printed on good paper. They are believed to have originated in the 1600s and were traditionally tacked on public bulletin boards.

Camera-ready copy: Laid-out pages of a book that is ready to be photographed (made into photographic printing plates) and printed. Compare to *electronic copy.*

Commercial press or publisher: A for-profit enterprise that usually has a broad list, national distribution and pays advances in the thousands. A commercial press might balance literary and commercial offerings, or might concentrate on commercial success.

Consignment: An agreement with a store that when it sells the item you leave with it you will receive back a percentage of the sale, usually around 50 percent.

Copyright: The right to publish a work or document.

Cover price: The price for which a book is offered for sale to the public.

Electronic copy: Copy for a book that is laid out in a computer program and is delivered to the printer on a disk. Compare to *camera-ready copy* and *hard copy.*

Hard copy: A document printed on paper. Compare to *electronic copy.*

Layout: Arrangement of pages and illustrations in a book.

List: The catalog of books offered by a press.

Literary or small press or publisher: Often a nonprofit business, the literary press usually has a small list, limited distribution, pays modest advances (hundreds rather than thousands of dollars) and focuses on literary fare rather than commercial. Compare to *commercial publisher.*

Midlist: Books on a publisher's list that are not expected to be major sellers. Such books are often supported by the success of the publisher's more commercial books.

Perfect-bound: See *square spine.*

Press: (1) A publisher of books or other printed materials; (2) a business that prints books and other materials, but does not "publish" them.

Publisher: A company that pays for the production and promotion of books and other printed materials.

Royalty: The returns paid to an author by a publisher of the author's work.

Saddle stitched: A booklet or pamphlet whose pages are folded in the middle and secured with staples or stitched with twine; compare to *square spine.* Saddle-stitched documents can be hand-bound by the publisher. Publishers can purchase an expensive hand saddle-stitch stapler. It has a "saddle" that accommodates the fold of the book, and makes stapling precise and easy.

Sans serif font: A type font that does not have serifs, the little tails at the ends of letter lines. Compare to *serif font.*

Serif font: A type font that has serifs, little tails at the ends of the letter lines. Serif fonts are easier to read than sans serif fonts. This book is printed in a serif font. Compare to *sans serif font.*

Square spine: A flat spine that is sewn and glued, also called "perfect-bound;" compare to *saddle stitched*. Square spines must usually be bound by a commercial bindery.

Subsidy or vanity publisher: A specialty publisher that does not pay for the production or promotion of its books. Those costs and fees for handling production and promotion are paid for by the author.

Web publishing: The publication of a document on a Web site rather than in hard copy.

Self-Publishing

If you are not interested in seeking a publisher for your work, you can consider publishing it yourself. Self-publishing has a long and proud history. The Scottish poet Robert Burns, the American poet Walt Whitman, the founder of Christian Science, Mary Baker Eddy, all self-published. More recently, *Mutant Message Down Under, The Celestine Prophecy* and *The Girls With the Grandmother Faces* are books that were originally self-published. Following word-of-mouth success, they were picked up by major publishers.

When you self-publish, you take on responsibility for all facets of the production and distribution of your work, including costs. You also get to keep all profits from sales.

To start your self-publishing adventure, read one or two books on self-publishing. Next, give your "press" a name. This lets your readers and buyers, including bookstores, know that you understand what it means to be a publisher. I self-published my first book, a collection of poems, and several issues of a literary magazine, under the aegis of Raspberry Press. I still use the name when I occasionally print a literary postcard or broadside. I am the editor and publisher of Raspberry Press.

Once you have your press name, you are ready to prepare your manuscript for publication. Start by going to a bookstore or a gift shop that carries local histories, and looking at books on the shelf where you would like your book to be. Notice the different shapes, sizes and bindings. This will help you think about the final form of your own book. Note, too, the type fonts used in most published books: You will want a basic serif font, such as the one used for this book. Sans-serif fonts are tiring to read, and best used only for short text such as headings and posters. Fancy fonts, such as scripts and shaded fonts, are also difficult to read.

If you are going to have a printer reproduce your book, you should talk to them early on about their services and their needs. The printer might have someone who can do layout for you or advise you on style decisions. You can also print your own book, either from your computer or using a photocopier. If you do your own, be sure to pay attention to the location of pages. For example, if you print your book on 8½″ × 14″ paper and fold the pages in the middle, you will get four pages from each sheet of paper. Only the sheet in the middle of the book will have the pages in consecutive order. Pages one and two will share a sheet of paper with the last two pages of the book. When looking at pages, also be aware that if you get four pages to a sheet of paper, your book will have a total number of pages divisible by four.

You can figure out most of what you need to know about printing a book by looking at other books and copying the formats you like. You should be especially aware of the copyright symbol and the statement on the back of the title page of most books. This statement, which must be in the book when you print it, insures that you retain copyrights to your story. It should look like this: "© Copyright Your Name, 200x." In most circumstances it is not necessary to register your copyright with the Library of Congress, though you may do so if you wish.

If you publish a book without the symbol and the statement, you can lose your copyright protection and the book can fall into the public domain. Published materials in the public domain can be printed by anyone without permission of or compensation to the author.

Once your book is off the press, you will want to distribute it for sale. You can offer it to friends, family and neighbors by printing a flyer about it. You can also take it to local bookstores and gift shops. They will often take books by local authors but usually on a consignment basis. This means they will not buy the book from you but will carry it on their shelves. When a copy of the book sells, you will receive a percentage of the sale, usually around 50 percent for consignment books. If you put your books out on consignment, be sure to keep good records of what is where, and check back with the stores every few months to collect your percentage of sales and to restock the book. Most stores will not contact you when a sale is made or when the supply is out.

Some stores will buy your book outright. The usual discount to the store is 40 percent of the cover price, meaning if the book sells for ten dollars they will buy it from you for six dollars. They then own the book and keep the proceeds when it sells. Although the publisher gets a lower percentage of the sale with outright sales, it is still a better deal because the publisher does not have to wait for subsequent sales in order to profit from the book.

In addition to putting your book out for sale, you might want to promote it in the local media, including newspapers and radio. There is one main thing to remember when you do this: The media does not care about you or your book. They care about their audience. If you have something of interest to their audience, they will then be interested in you. Always present your book in the light of a news hook—a connection to current events. If your community is about to celebrate an anniversary, your book can be promoted for its value as a social document. If your book is about your mother and grandmother, you can present it as a human interest story for Mother's Day. The media is always looking for stories. Make it easy for them to use yours.

Seeking a Publisher

You might want to seek a literary or commercial publisher for your book. As with self-publishing, the search for a publisher can be a job in its own right, but, as with self-publishing, the rewards can be most satisfying.

You can start your search by learning a bit about presses that publish memoirs. Go to a bookstore, and find the shelf where you think your book should be. Look at the books there, and make notes about who published them. Keep an eye out especially for less well-known presses: They are more likely to consider work from a writer who is not previously published. You can also look for potential publishers in *Writer's Market* and similar books. These references are published annually and give complete information on what publishing houses are looking for and how to contact them. Most libraries carry current editions of these books.

Once you have identified some presses that might be interested in your manuscript, you can contact them for their writers' guidelines. Sometimes you can get them by calling the press, sometimes you have to write. Some presses now have their writers' guidelines online, so you can check there, too.

The guidelines will tell you if the press accepts manuscripts from authors or only through agents. They will also tell you if they want to see the whole manuscript or only the proposal. It is best to follow the protocols they set forward.

If you are asked to send a proposal—the usual way to approach a publisher—write a one-page letter describing you and your book. Start with a paragraph that broaches your subject: ''In the 1940s, we children called it Crookety Lane. It was a dirt road that went nowhere but led us into the land of childhood make-believe. Today it is a freeway crossing. My memoir, *Blue Pond, Green Meadow,* tells how the change came to be.''

Your second paragraph should say why the press should publish your book. Refer to similar books on its list, and tell why its readers will also be interested in your book. The third paragraph should say why you should be the one to write this book. Give any professional credentials you have, and relate it to the experiences in your memoir: ''I have taught third grade for twenty years and understand what childhood means to us.''

In the fourth and closing paragraph, you can say if the memoir is complete or when it will be ready. You can also say that a chapter of the memoir and the table of contents or an outline are enclosed. Do not thank them in advance for their attention. ''Sincerely'' is an appropriate sign-off.

When you send the letter, send one or two chapters, the outline and a one-page resumé of your education and job experience, even if neither are related to writing or to your story. Everyone likes to be in good company.

It will be easier to sell your memoir if it is complete. It is unusual today for a novice writer to be given a contract for a work in-progress. It is not unusual, however, for literary or smaller commercial presses to take on new writers. There are many midsize publishers in this country that do a good job of production and promotion of books. There are probably some in your region, and that is a good place to start your search for a publisher. As with the media, regional publishers are usually interested in a news hook, and a local author writing about a local subject constitutes such a hook.

What you can expect from your publisher depends a great deal on the size of the publishing house. If you sign with a national publisher, you can expect a modest promotional budget and an advance in the low to mid thousands of dollars. If you sign with a smaller press, whether commercial or literary, you can expect a restricted promotional budget and an advance from the hundreds to the low thousands. Even with a large press, much of the promotion will fall to you, at your own expense. Most publishers today promote their books directly to bookstores, but arrangements for media contacts and promotional readings are up to the author.

Whether you sign with a small house or a large one, you will be offered a publishing contract. You should consider the contract carefully: In it you sell certain rights to the work you created. You have the right to ask questions about each item and to request that some items be altered or removed. If an editor says to you, "Oh, that's standard," you still don't have to accept it. If they have gone this far with you—have offered you a contract—they are not going to change their minds and go away in a huff just because you want to change a few items. In the end, you might not succeed in getting the changes, but there is little or no harm in asking for them.

In general, you should expect an advance that would cover the first year's royalties on your book. The publisher will have a pretty good idea of what that might be. The advance is usually paid in two or three installments. If it is paid in two, you receive half on signing and half on completion of the manuscript, including revisions agreed to by you and an editor. Three-part advances are usually paid one-third on signing, one-third on completion and one-third on publication.

Your contract will also state your royalties. Larger presses usually offer 10 percent of the cover price on hardcover books, escalating up to 12 to 15 percent with increasing sales, and 6½ to 8½ percent of the cover price on paperbacks, again with an increased royalty with increased sales. Smaller presses often offer royalties based on net sales rather than on cover price. That royalty is usually around 12 to 15 percent.

In addition to royalty rates and other items, your contract will state what rights to your work you are selling. It is a good idea to be stingy about this. There are few circumstances that would justify giving up all rights to your work. Rather, you should only sell the rights that the publisher will use. If they will do a paperback, do not sell them hardcover rights. If they will not try to sell the book to a movie producer, do not sell them movie rights. A negotiator might say to you, "Well, we never use those anyway." You can then say that they therefore do not need to have them. If an item is a sticking point for a negotiator, they will tell you so, and you can decide if it's worth it to back off.

These comments should give you some idea of what you might expect in a publishing contract, but if you get to the point of signing one, you would be wise to learn more about literary contracts before putting pen to paper. There are books available, intellectual property attorneys can help, and organizations such as the

National Writers Union offer free contract advice to their members. Your book is your intellectual property, and you should be as careful with its sale as you would be with the sale of a house.

Publishing in Magazines and Journals

Parts of your memoir might be publishable in outlets other than book form. Go to the public library or browse *Writer's Market*, or a similar reference book, and find the names of magazines and journals that publish personal essays. Obtain their writers' guidelines. Look at several back issues. If you find publications that might be interested in a chapter or essay from your memoir, send it to them, using a cover letter similar in form to the book proposal described earlier. With magazine publication, you are likely to find many readers who you would not reach with a book, and the publication credit will look good to book publishers. As with book publishing, look first for local and regional periodical publishers that might be interested in your story.

Small Presses and Magazines

When searching for a publisher for your memoir, or for parts of it, investigate the rich and varied world of the "small press." These publishers of books and magazines are in the business for the pleasure of bringing words and books to print. They rarely make a profit. Recompense for publication is often in free copies rather than in royalties.

You can find local and regional small presses by asking your local art council or a similar organization. You can also subscribe to local or regional literary newsletters and to *Poets and Writers* magazine (http://www.pw.org). *P&W* runs classified ads from small presses looking for submissions. My memoir *Girl to Woman*, published by Astarte Shell Press, came about when I answered an ad in *P&W*.

Subsidy or Vanity Publishing

If at any point in your discussion with a publisher you are asked to contribute to the cost of producing your book, you are probably dealing with a subsidy (vanity) publisher. If so, proceed with caution. Subsidy publishers usually publish the manuscript of anyone willing to pay their fees. The fees run two to four times more than it would cost the author to self-publish.

In return for the fees, the subsidy publisher handles all aspects of production and usually does minimal promotion. They also usually retain some rights to the books that are printed, and if the books do not sell, you might be asked if you want to purchase them—i.e., pay for them again, when you already paid for their printing. If you don't buy them back, they might be shredded.

Subsidy publishers do lend their name to your book, but you can acquire the same credibility by creating a publisher name for your self-publishing venture.

If you do want to proceed with a subsidy publisher, have a knowledgeable writer or lawyer, preferably an intellectual property rights lawyer, review the contract before you sign it. You should also compare your subsidy costs to the costs of self-publishing.

Electronic Publishing

The printed page is no longer the only publishing format. It is now possible for presses and individuals to publish on Web sites. Many of the concerns regarding hard copy publishing stand true for Web publishing. If you are self-publishing, look around at other book sites so that you can put forth a professional-looking e-book. Be sure to claim your copyright on the site, using the conventional copyright statement: "© Copyright Your Name, 200x." As with hard copy publishing, under most circumstances it is not necessary to register your copyright with the Library of Congress, though you may do so if you wish.

If an e-publisher wants to publish your memoir online, refer to the concerns expressed in the section on Subsidy or Vanity Publishing. You can probably do as a good a job or better publishing your own work on the Web, and you would retain all rights and profits for yourself. If you wish to pursue being published by an e-publisher, talk about it with someone you trust who is knowledgeable about e-commerce. You can also find information on e-publishing in literary magazines and newsletters. Sometimes these are available at local libraries.

Whether you publish online yourself or through an e-publisher, remember that text on a Web site can be read and copied for free. You or your publisher should look into protecting your text by offering it for a fee through a download process. While it is true that someone who pays the fee and downloads your text can then copy it and give it away, you will at least have provided one line of protection for your intellectual property.

Literary Agents

Literary agents are book brokers. If they accept your manuscript, they try to sell it to a publisher. In recompense, they usually get 15 percent of your royalties for as long as the book is in print by the same publisher.

You can approach an agent the same way you approach a publisher: Present a proposal and sample chapters. Although some agents now charge a reading fee for considering a manuscript, this is not yet common practice, and you should avoid such an arrangement.

The safest way to find an agent is through a writer or an arts organization. If you locate an agent other than through personal contact, ask for references and check them out. Once you settle on an agent, ask for your financial agreement in writing. Make sure it states the agent's percentage of your royalties and lists expenses that you might be responsible for, such as photocopying and postage. Some agents don't like to bother with this, but you should insist. A letter countersigned by both of you can suffice.

Experiments

1. Self-Publishing. To get a feel for self-publishing, try printing a broadside or a pamphlet of part of your memoir. The broadside could be a photograph of a place with a one-paragraph description of it for a caption. This could later be used as part of a flyer to promote the book. A chapter of your book could be made into a pamphlet and used for a holiday gift.

2. Learning About Publishing. To learn more about

the publishing world, go to your local library and look for books on writing and publishing. While there, look in the nonfiction section for books that might be similar to yours. Make note of the publishers, the shape of the books, reviews of the book—anything that might help you better understand publishing.

3. *Learning About Being an Author.* If you have access to a published writer—directly, through friends or friends of friends—try to arrange a visit with them. Ask them for advice and help. It is a good way to learn the publishing ropes. You can also go to literary readings, join a writers group, join an arts organization or go to a writers' conference. That's where the writers are, so that's where you should be.

Afterword

Reading a book about writing is, I imagine, a lot like reading a book about swimming: In the end, reading is not enough. To learn to swim, you have to dive into the water, get wet, sink frequently, and gasp for air now and then. Finally, if you are both diligent and lucky, you will come to know how to stay on top of the water, and you will develop a stroke and rhythm of your own invention that will get you back to shore.

Because I believe that is how we come to be writers— by inventing the process for ourselves, each and every one of us—I don't like to give much advice about writing. I prefer to encourage, and to offer a word here and there about technique. I avoid the word *should*. I don't believe discipline has much to do with writing: Most of us write out of passion and desire, not because we are supposed to.

I believe most new writers don't realize how much latitude and power they have. A young woman said to me once, "But if I write about that, I'll have to make it all up." "That's what we do," I replied. "We make it all up, even when we are telling the truth."

However, I am willing to give advice about some things. I think most writers today should be working on word processors, not typewriters. The computer is tremendously liberating, and it is good for all of us to learn new things now and then. I also think e-mail is a good thing—it brings people together in a new way, offering quick correspondence. I sometimes exchange four or five e-mails a day with one other person. It's like having tea together—the conversation is usually mundane and therefore sweet in a special way.

I like the World Wide Web, and any one who wants to work at writing in more than a casual way needs to learn how to use it.

I think one of the hardest things for new writers is to claim authorship of their work. Most are willing to say that they are writing something but would not deign to call themselves "writers." Until you are willing to do that, your work is in jeopardy—not from external forces but from internal forces. If you can't muster it, try to figure out why. Hang out with other writers. Take classes. Practice saying it. "I am a writer."

Writers who work on a computer for the first time are also timid with their machines. We must be firm with our computers and make them work for us. Still, they do have powers we must deal with: Computers can eat our work. Learn about saving and backing up your writing, and do it diligently. Set your word processing software to auto-save every five minutes. Then do a manual save at the end of every paragraph or so. At the end of a work session, back up your work on another disk, or at least in another file, and print out a hard copy of the day's writing. You do not have to learn the importance of this the way the rest of us did, by losing hours of work to the fickle world of electricity.

In addition to saving your work electronically, save your hard copies and your notes. Don't throw away anything until six months after the book is in print. Get a big cardboard box, put it at the end of your desk and drop all paper into it, whether you think you'll need it again or not.

Writing is born out of passion and desire, but it is bred, brought up, in obsession and compulsion. Feed your drive to persist. Damn your fears. Claim your writing as your own. When you get stuck, when you freeze up, when your mind goes as empty as a sky during drought, close your eyes and remember why you wanted to write this book in the first place.

Now, stop reading, sit yourself down at your keyboard, and don't get up until you have committed at least one good sentence, one that breathes sensory detail, to the future of your memoir.

Memoir Reader

Writers Reading

The first six essays in this appendix were written by students in my writing classes at Bemidji State University in northern Minnesota. The last is an essay of my own. I include them here not to encourage you to write a certain way but rather to encourage you to look at writing—yours and that of others—in a certain way. The introductory passage to each section of essays might help you recognize how the language of a writer contributes to the overall effect of an essay. You might then be able to better recognize the way you utilize language in your own writing. It is important, I think, not to write like others but to recognize that you have a style, a voice, a way of speaking that is unique to you, and to be able to talk about your own writing the way you talk about the writing of others.

The assignments for these essays grew out of class discussions about writing, and about the use of imagery and the senses in writing. In a similar way, the experiments at the end of each chapter of this book evolved from the discussion in the chapter and can serve as writing assignments.

Snapshots

Sometimes our memoirs, our memories, spill out of us in long stories that are like movies, full of places and characters and moving from here to there. Other times a single event reveals itself to us in a snapshot, an intense or poignant moment that stands on its own.

In these three stories, the authors write about single events in their lives. They all use details to bring the memory alive on the page, but they each use them in different ways.

In her story "Sunrise/Sunset," Jennifer A. Woestehoff brings us into her story with the use of details. Instead of dialogue, however, she describes objects that are easy for us to imagine, such as cement steps, ice cubes and Kool-Aid. She also uses evocative language—"the shock of blue sky"—and personifications that invite us into the emotions of the experience: "darkness embraces our bodies" and "the shy earth."

Jeff Poenix, in "A Burning Sphere of Fire," also uses evocative descriptions to create the mood of his experience. Unlike the first story, however, Jeff invites us into his thoughts rather than into his life. In fact, throughout the piece, he pushes his life away, choosing instead to enter a moment and even yearning to remain in it longer.

Liu Wei's detailed dialogue in "The Royal Road" invites us to walk the tunnel with him and his friend. Their conversation is enhanced by descriptions of the tunnel and the landscape. It is also enhanced by descriptions of the food at food stalls along the way, especially by Liu Wei's description of the bitter tea they drink toward the end of their journey and by his contemplation on their experience.

The tone of each story is determined in part by details and descriptions, but it is also affected by the writer's word choices, and by sentence lengths and structures. The first time you read the stories, you might just read them, letting their flavors roll over you. Then, go back and read them again, this time making note of details, description, words and sentences. Perhaps you can tell how these elements contribute to your response to the stories. Later, you might try looking at your own writings the same way.

Sunrise/Sunset

JENNIFER A. WOESTEHOFF

Mike, my best friend, is leaving for the army tomorrow, and the black sky of midnight hangs over my head as we say our final good-byes. I sit tall next to Mike on the cold, cement steps of his house, and I feel tears making puddles in my eyes as we begin to talk and reminisce about our high school days. When he mentions the time he locked me in my locker I can't help but laugh, and when he whispers words about our trip to the Boundary Waters a permanent smile is sewn onto my face.

As we sit side by side I feel free because I am next to the friend who lets me exist. Mike makes me feel like a queen, and I'm in power of the whole world. At the same time I smell the wind in my hair, and up above I see the stars that lose themselves in a random mess. The night spills its velvet stain over us, and the darkness embraces our bodies.

The fullness of my heart pleads to burst as we discuss our first loves, our first losses and the beauty of our mutual friends. Time ceases to exist, and I'm glad no clocks need winding. I think our night will last forever, and I plan to invent new stars since they will fade with light. I want the scent of Mike's cologne to remain heavy upon my flesh, and I hope our voices will always sing in harmony.

At one point Mike's mom steals the spotlight and hands us ice-cold Kool-Aid. The melted ice cubes soothe my throat from laughing and talking more than usual. Her long, lanky body hovers over our heads, protecting us from the light I know will soon shine.

When I'm again left alone with Mike we sing our favorite song, "You've Lost That Loving Feeling," and we quote lines from our favorite movie, *Top Gun*. We race down the driveway as I hope to finally beat Mike, although I fail, and we shout out our greatest inside jokes.

Suddenly, I see light that appears as pink fabric stretching out in the shy earth, and a blond flame peaks through. Then a round, red disk springs up, and light tiptoes among the silver branches in front of me. The dry heat warms my bones, and the shock of blue sky makes me mad. My heart turns to seaweed as the reality of moving on and meeting new friends hits me. We will lose touch eventually, we will walk different paths, and the scent of Mike's skin will fade in my mind. I give Mike one last hug, and I lightly step away from the door. As I drive away, I wish I would have drawn a compass around Mike's belly that would lead him to me again, but now it's too late since the bright, blazing sun will blind me if I turn back.

A Burning Sphere of Fire
(and it burns, burns, burns . . .)

JEFF POENIX

Another day draws nearer to its end, marked once again by the settling of the sun on the far western horizon. I drive east on the interstate, headed home after an exhausting trip, so worn out that the only things on my mind are the comforts of my nice warm bed and the impending sleep that will soon ensue upon my arrival. I look back over my right shoulder, across the sprawling South Dakota landscape and am immediately immersed in the shimmering glow of that sphere of fire as it settles into the landscape for another night's sleep. I can't help but feel slightly jealous, as if it is mocking me—telling me that it is able to sleep while I can't.

It is not long before I have to look away from that spectacular sight and concentrate on the task at hand, but the image of that sun, as if it were burning a hole right into that South Dakota prairie, is still emblazoned in my mind. I can't help thinking about that orb as it sheds its crepuscular light upon the landscape.

I wish that I could prolong this event, and instead of running away from the sun, I was running toward it. I wish that I could keep it within my view and bask in its amber rays until the day comes when either it or I am no more. Although the sun is setting, and although I will once again have to go through another dark, cold night without the comforting rays of the evening sun, I take solace in the fact that the rotation of the Earth all but guarantees me yet another peek of it the following day. Until then, I guess I'll just keep on heading east, dreaming about tomorrow.

The Royal Road

LIU WEI

It was in my hometown—Chongqing, China, and I was ten that year.

"At noon when the class is over, go home straight. Don't linger on the streets," my father enjoined me when I was going to school. "I know," I responded in a low, protracted voice, stepping out of my home, bag in hand.

At noon, when the last class in the morning was over, my friend Yang and I stepped out of our classroom. Immediately we were under the glare of the summer sun.

"Which way shall we take to go home today?" I asked Yang, who was also my neighbor.

"Yesterday we climbed the upper hill to go home. The day before yesterday we circled most of the football field to go home. What new way shall we take today?" he sent my question back.

It did not baffle me. Our city was a mountain city. Between two places, besides the different ways in horizontal direction, there were also different ways in vertical direction.

"Why can't we try the tunnel?" I suggested.

"Oh, yeah, we can do that."

I knew today we would have a good way to go, for the way home via the tunnel would be the longest among all the ways.

We passed a peddler who was selling red grapes. I dared not take a close look at the grapes that would activate every taste bud of mine, for my parents did not give me money for them. We passed other candies on the street as well. Under the dense green foliage of a huge banyan tree, an old woman was selling sweet ice, which attracted numerous kids scrambling to get one. I didn't follow the fashion because the sweet ice would make my hands sticky, which I could not bear. On our long way home, there was no place to wash my hands.

When we were passing the huge banyan tree that served as the landmark of the intersection of the road, instead of turning right toward our homes, we advanced straight forward toward places beyond our knowledge.

"Yang, today we take a new way. What shall we call it?" I asked.

"Let's call it 'Tunnel Way.' "

"No, that sounds commonplace. Think of something special. How about 'The Longest Way'?" I proposed.

"No, we'd better not call it the 'The Longest Way.' Think one day when we discover a longer one than this, then what should we do?"

"Oh, yes. You're right," I acknowledged. The superlative could not describe our mood.

We continued thinking about the name and continued on our way. We descended about one hundred steps to the entrance of the tunnel. My feet could step on the head of my shadow on the ground. Yeah, it was noon now, the sun was right overhead. My city was known as a furnace in summer. I felt the sultry air baking my skin, and the sweat was oozing out of it. I didn't care. I focused upon walking the way.

At the entrance, I saw the tunnel was dim inside without lamps. It was straight but too long for me to discern its other end—our exit. We entered it. We wanted to see how long we should grope in the dimness.

"This is the first time I walk in the tunnel," Yang said.

"Me, too."

Inside the tunnel, the vehicles were passing through it one after another sending incessant noise to our ears, which made it difficult for us to hear each other. Moreover, the air inside the tunnel was stuffy and dusty. We spared talking to each other and concentrated on our walking. On my way, all that I saw was the murky rock on the two sides and the top of the tunnel.

We walked forward. More vehicles passed, more noise produced, more dust stirred by the vehicles, more dusty air taken into my lungs, more steps made, more distance unfolded before us. The scene did not seem to change. We seemed unlikely to walk out of the tunnel. Looking at the murky rock over my head, I thought that before I walked out of it, if the rock suddenly collapsed, what should I become? Should I be crushed to powder or be maimed in agony unable to move? This was too horrible for me to think of. I repelled the vision.

We kept moving our legs mechanically forward. I lost the concept of how much time passed.

By and by, a dim-lighted circle loomed in front. We made more steps toward it, and it became clearer.

"Finally, we are going to walk out of the tunnel," Yang said, consoled.

"Yeah, it's too long. Next time we might not take it."

After quite a time of walking, we found ourselves under the glaring sunbeam again. Now the sunbeam seemed able to penetrate my already heated and tired body.

When we were ascending another hundred steps toward our homes, we stopped at a peddler who was selling bitter tea. We both spent two cents to buy a glass of it. It tasted so good. Every nerve of mine was massaged by it. My heat and tiredness dispersed. I hadn't found that bitter tea could taste as such before. I believed nobody else might know it; otherwise it wouldn't be so cheap. Only we knew it. Suddenly a whim occurred to me.

"Shall we call today's way 'Royal Road'?" I proposed.

" 'Royal Road?' Sounds strange."

"Think what a way we have made today. Nobody else goes the way for the reason we did. It's different. It's a privilege. Only we know it," I explained.

"Yeah, it is. Other people don't know it; they don't know that bitter tea is to be drunk after such a long walk."

"No, they don't know. We don't tell them, do we?"

"Of course not."

Our homes were already in sight. We discussed some words to avert our parents' interrogations for our late homecoming.

Moving Pictures

The two stories in this section, so different in subject, have several things in common. First, the reader is taken along through a series of related events that have a culminating moment. This is different than a story, such as Woestehoff's in Snapshots, where earlier events are brought in as examples, but are not themselves the story.

Second, they are both filled with visual details, and often those details suggest ways to think about other things in the stories. In Erlys J. Moore's story, the episode of the failed stenciling project echoes the muss of the girl's efforts to bring her own life into focus. In Kathleen C. Headbird's story, the cookstove with its strong legs echoes the character of the mother and the packsack the character of the father.

Third, the titles of both pieces can mean more than one thing. "A Music Lesson," Moore's title, is less easy to sort out. There is the lesson that the girl learned and the one the woman knows from looking back. There is also the lesson the reader might learn, and probably others that I have not yet caught on to. Headbird's title, "The Sunrise and Sunset of Maggie Odaanis," can refer to the literal sunrise and sunset of a given day, but also to the larger sunrise and sunset of her life and even to her husband's role in her life.

The additional readings of these titles, of course, do

not occur to us until after we have read the stories. Even writers are surprised sometimes by the multiple ways an image or a phrase enlarges the stories they tell. As you read these essays, and your own, make note of objects or phrases that lend themselves to enhancing a scene or a character or even the overall import of the story.

A Music Lesson

ERLYS J. MOORE

My twelfth Christmas was quickly approaching. The familiar questioning from my parents of what I wanted from Santa had begun. They knew, and I knew, Santa did not bring my gifts, but they still insisted on playing the game. My dad drove me to Moorhead one Saturday morning before Christmas. Moorhead was the closest large town to our small town of 150. We parked near the Coast to Coast store on Main Avenue. It was a hardware store, but in those days it was more like a variety store carrying much more than just hardware. Its two large window displays were brightly lit with a rainbow of intertwined lights. Stencils and snow foam had painted flocked pictures of Santa, sleighs, trees, ornaments and gifts. I remembered my attempt to stencil two of our windows at home. I had taped the paper stencils upon the windows, shook the spray can and carefully released the white chemical foam contents. Oops! I must have sprayed too much because when I tried to remove the taped stencils, the only picture left upon the pane was a white-out blizzard. I wondered how the store had got its pictures to be so perfect.

My dad opened the door for me. I entered with one goal in mind. I wanted to find a stereo. I didn't want a large stereo system. All I wanted was a simple stereo with speakers, an automatic needle arm that could easily play 33⅓ vinyl albums and 45 rpm records. I did have a record player that was mahogany brown, about two feet square and that laid flat, opening like a suitcase. The only speakers it had were several small round holes punched through the surface in one corner of the flat suitcase. It was a simple, basic record player that I had received six years earlier. I was approaching my teenage years in a few months, and I just had to have something a little bit more automatic with modern features.

I remembered spotting a dark object outlined by silvery details as I had entered the store; I was sure it had been a stereo. I didn't walk right up to it at first because my dad was alongside of me. It wouldn't have been proper for me to run to the first thing I saw and loudly exclaim that this was what I wanted for Christmas. I was taught not to ask for something, but I was allowed to answer if I had been asked. My dad went about his business and so did I.

I walked carefully through each aisle looking at the crowded shelves on both sides of me. The toys were all fighting for their rightful space. It seemed each of them was battling for the front row hoping to attract an eye of a future owner. Some of those toys did their duty very well; I was a magnet, forcefully pulled toward a few of them. But I couldn't look at them, let alone say I wanted one for Christmas, because I was twelve years old and that meant I was too big for toys.

The clocks began to signal a new hour. Dad probably was about done with his business, and he would soon be asking if I saw anything I liked, so I quickly walked to the front of the store. I desperately wanted to find that front row with that questionable object. There on my left was a single shelf lined with soft wisps of cotton sprinkled with glitter. Sitting on top of that blanket of snow was the dark object with a shining front panel of silver knobs. I knew this was what I wanted, this was my stereo. It was a black General Electric stereo that stood upright with the turntable folding down. It had two speakers, one on each side. These speakers could even be removed a short distance from the unit with a simple turn of a silver brace. The turntable had three speeds. It also had an automatic arm and the ability to hold more than one record at a time. Yes! This was the gift I wanted for Christmas.

My dad soon approached and asked if there was anything I saw that I wanted. I remember being very hesitant, almost fearful in my admitting my dream gift. I slowly allowed the words to form and spill from my mouth. He asked if I was sure and if I had looked all around, maybe there was something else I might want. I assured him that this was really all I wanted. A salesperson asked if he could be of any assistance. My dad began talking with him, asking the usual consumer questions. I couldn't tell from my dad's expression or his words if he was in favor of my choice; I certainly didn't dare question him. He cleared his throat and said it was time to get going. We left the Coast to Coast store, walked to our car, got in and drove home; nothing more was said about the stereo.

My mom was an overflowing well of questions once we got home. She wanted to know where we had gone, what we had done and especially what we had bought. She seemed to enjoy Christmas with all of its surprises, but her biggest thrill was if she could get you to answer what gifts she might be getting. Christmas seasons were a game with her, consisting of teasing and torturing, all in good fun, of course. Mom would just love to tell me that I would only be getting two lumps of coal wrapped up in a box, or she would continuously list several items that she knew I would not like. Since I always received separate gifts from Mom and Dad, I persistently asked her if she knew what Dad was going to give me this year. I just had to know if I was going to receive that stereo, because if not, I wanted to be prepared for the letdown. Her answer was different this year, there were not any hints as in the past, all she repeatedly said was that she didn't know.

Christmas Eve morning I awoke with impatient excitement. There would be stacks of gifts to open after dinner, but my curiosity was only regarding the one big present sitting under the tree from Dad. The day progressed on the clock by the seconds, not minutes nor hours, but ticked away by the seconds. Finally, after dinner we moved into the living room, where Mom, Dad and I would begin to open our carefully wrapped gifts. I handed out all the gifts, stacking a mountain before my chair. I awaited for the nod of approval that I could begin. I wanted to know immediately what was in that one extremely large box, but I also wanted to enjoy the suspense a little longer, so I began with a few small packages. I was being a lot more patient than what most other twelve-year-olds could tolerate. Then, when I absolutely could not take it any longer, I walked over to that one, lonely, large, wrapped gift.

I heard words coming from behind me as I began ripping off the paper. I think I heard, "Be careful, maybe something will jump out at you," followed by, "Maybe it's not what you want, don't be too disappointed," and finally, "Why don't you leave that one until morning." I didn't care what words were floating in my ears, I just wanted to discover the contents of that box! It sure was the right-sized box for the stereo, it sure felt heavy enough for the stereo, but as I opened the final flap of the box, my eyes played a horrible trick. I saw a tight, colored object. It was large, square shaped and made out of oak. I proceeded to lift open the wooden lid, and my eyes revealed an old-time, windup, Victor phonograph, the metal crank laid upon the green, felt turntable. I was horrified! I heard spear-sharp laughing. A smoldering fire sparked across my face. The salty drops streamed over my lips. I bolted for the bathroom, the only door with a lock. I locked myself safe within the four walls, where I unlocked the flow of hurt, shame and disappointment.

Above my wails, Mom's voice drifted through the door saying that Dad has gone outside to bring in my real present and I was to come out to open it. I refused. I don't think I ever had been so disappointed before in my life. I didn't like the laughter. I didn't like the joke. I didn't trust what was next to come. I wouldn't leave the bathroom. My dad had gotten mad at my refusal to come out, so he went outside to his shop. Mom told me that I'd better come out now!

I came out and slowly walked back into the living room. There was a new large gift waiting to be opened. I really was fearful of what that box may contain also, so I opened it one small tear at a time. I would have squealed with delight, happiness and pleasure, but the pain from the moment before was still too fresh, like an open wound. The General Electric stereo from the Coast to Coast store was now gleaming before my eyes, just waiting to be opened and played. My dad came into the living room as I began to check it out. He made a gruff comment about the value of the antique phonograph compared to the new plastic stereo. He said the Victor tabletop version was made in 1914, and it was the first flat disk phonograph. He stressed that the General Electric stereo would lose its value, but the old oak Victor would only increase in its value. I respected him enough to hear his words, but I was only interested in testing out my new modern object.

My dad firmly believed that old items were always more durable than any new advanced items. He told me to mark his words, one day I would come to believe what he said about the Edison's value increasing and outlasting the other one. Well, I used that new modern stereo through all my teenage years where it received a lot of wear and tear. I continued to use it until I was twenty-two years old, until I purchased another new, more modern stereo. My mom took the General Electric stereo and used it for another eight years. My parents still have the stereo located somewhere, but they are not sure that it works.

I still have my Victor tabletop phonograph, and it does work. The last time I tried using it was a few months ago. All I had to do was crank it up, move the brass lever down into the play position and place the heavy metal arm with its needle down onto the thick old record. Soon the scratchy, familiar crackling sound of the first flat disk music drifted out of the front panel. It has proved its durability and increased value. Over the years, it has become priceless to me, but I will always remember it was at the expense of a joke.

The Sunrise and Sunset of Maggie Odaanis
KATHLEEN C. HEADBIRD

I remember how I felt so honored when you invited me along with you to check your trap line and your snares.

You never gave your gunnysack packsack much thought, but I did. I watched as you picked it up from beneath the huge old wood cookstove with its long, sleek, strong legs. That is where you stored the firewood also. Alongside the wood somewhere is where your old packsack laid as if it were resting for the night.

It was always early morning when we headed out for the woods. During breakfast you and Mom speculated whether there would be rabbits in your snares. According to your conversation, it seemed to depend on certain factors, like if it had been cold enough the night before, the rabbits would have run, thus the chances were better. If there had been moonlight the night before, the chances of getting a rabbit were slim. I understood the rabbits did not run if it had been a bright moonlit night.

And so we'd leave. You would trudge through the snow, breaking a path for me. You reminded me as if you were doing a traditional Indian dance with your feet, in your effort to make it easier for me. I felt the love you had for me spread throughout my being, warming me. I watched with pride as you put your hand up to your brow, protecting your eyes from the bright early morning sunrise.

You looked in the direction of your snare, hanging from the underbrush on sticks you had set up just so. Yep, there it was, our evening meal.

You then showed me how to reset the snare, never saying that it was meant for me to learn, just showing me, never stating any expectations, just showing me.

On days when you headed for the woods alone, I watched from the window until you were clearly out of sight. I then waited, anticipating the gunnysack packsack would be filled with little animals whose lives were given up to sustain our family.

You walked across the lake into town where you traded the hides for a little money, which would fill the gunnysack packsack with Mom's sugar and flour, and maybe a pound of hamburger for soup. And, of course, some oranges and bananas for me.

Many times Mom and I waited for your return from town. I knew what Mom was anticipating, that you had run into the guys. But Mom waited patiently, until the sun was setting into the horizon. "Come on, my girl," Mom would say. Mom led me into the woods where she selected a dry tree, then she and I pulled it home. It was at these times that Mom taught me about the different kinds of trees and their purposes. When we reached the house, I sat on the tree to steady it as Mom sawed it into firewood. We both carried it in and placed it beneath the old wood cookstove, beneath its long, sleek, strong legs.

Just as we could barely see, we spotted you coming up the path, gunnysack packsack in your hand, not on your back. Both Mom and I knew what kept you. It was as though even the setting sun had known.

Frames

Often our life stories come to us through the memory of images, events or objects. Then, when we tell the stories, we can infer from them an idea or a value: A story of a picnic at the beach might imply that picnics are fun and that it is good for us to be out in nature. Other times, we come to a story through an idea, which we then illustrate with examples of images, events or objects.

In "Instant Karma," Jessica Higgins's subject is the idea of reincarnation. She uses the topic to address a series of experiences in her own life, ones in which she compares herself to various animals. The humorous details of the story are based on Higgins's shortcomings as a physically adept human being. The failure of reincarnation to explain her tendencies echoes the failures she relates in the story.

The subject of Willow Kraeplin's "What Death Really

Means'' is clearly stated in the title, in a brief preface and in her closing comments. The subject is also stated throughout the story about her grandmother, holding up the details and images the way a trellis holds up the stems and branches of a vining rose.

Of course, it is not usually possible or necessary to say whether a story is strictly an idea illustrated with experiences, or experiences shaped into ideas. In most writing, the abstract (idea) and the concrete (experience) flow in and out of each other, the way they do in our lives. When you read these stories a second time, watch for the shifts from abstract to concrete and back. You can look for this play of the mind in your own work, too.

Instant Karma

JESSICA HIGGINS

In my past life I was a monkey. That's according to an Internet site where you answer a series of questions, and it tallies the answers and produces your past life. I'm fairly sure it's not accurate because if I had been a monkey in my past life, I'd like to believe I would have been able to hold onto the bars a little better in the first grade. I was performing a traditional cherry drop when my body stopped obeying the commands of my brain and I went sailing. I came down hard, biting through my tongue and popping out a tooth. The tooth actually landed in Mary Cloud's shirt pocket, and I still have a loose flap on my tongue. They can't stitch your tongue.

So, I think the monkey business is slightly inaccurate, even if I do like the idea. I was also told once by a magazine prediction that I used to be an otter. Like the monkey, it is a fun, outgoing creature, but once again I believe they missed the mark. The magazine told me that otters adapted to land and sea life, easily making the transition from one to the other. But they don't know about swimming lessons in the third grade.

I had landed myself in the advanced class by holding my breath while doing the front crawl. The truth was that I really had never gotten the breathing down right and just found it easier to fake it. This was fine for short distances but became a problem for lap swimming. I didn't tell anyone this secret, thus feeding my own anxiety and giving myself an ulcer at age eight. In this advanced class, all we did was swim back and forth across the deep end. Holding my breath for this long made me dizzy, and I often worried I was on my way to the bottom of the pool.

But I managed. Managed at the rate of literally making myself sick with worry. It was the morning before my final swim test, the test that would graduate me to an even more advanced class, and it was more than I could take. I found myself puking breakfast out in the back seat of Grandpa's Cadillac. It was then that I could no longer keep my secret. I couldn't breathe on the front crawl, and someone was going to have to scrape me off the bottom of the deep end at the Aviation Club. I missed my test and never made the swim team that summer.

My mother says she doesn't believe in past lives. But she once went to a seminar where some guy asked you questions about your children, and he told you what animal each are most like and what that means about you. I was a flamingo, a quiet, subdued creature unless in a pack, and then I guess they're quite boisterous. Anyway, I don't think this is fitting at all, because I associate balance with flamingos. And quite frankly, balance is not one of my key features. I have to recall the time involving the trash can.

In my eleventh grade English class, I was seated right next to the wastebasket. One morning after deciding my gum had become old, I leaned over and spit the gum out. I can't say I took much aim; it was a lazy effort that resulted in a short spit. The gum landed just shy of the trash can on the floor next to me. I contemplated the gum. Should I lean over and pick it up, or pretend I never saw it? I was deciding to go with the latter when I raised my gaze and locked eyes with Mr. Terry. His look told me everything I needed to know.

So, I leaned over my desk, one of those contraptions where the desk is attached to the seat with an aluminum bar, and my lean turned into a fall directed for the wastebasket. My head and right arm went straight into the garbage, while the rest of my body and desk were all over the place. If this weren't a scene in itself, Mr. Terry tried to catch me, but my forward motion took us both down. I later had to work the gum out of the carpet because my knee had fused the two together.

I'd like to think I was once an animal gifted with grace and dexterity, but I'm afraid all my actions lead in the opposite direction. Like the time I superglued my finger to my nose. Or the instance with the barbecue and my eyebrows. After mentioning those, I can't leave off shutting my finger in my locker in the ninth grade or falling down the stairs in the seventh. This isn't even a catalog of my accidents with motorized vehicles.

So, if I were to pick the animal I was in my past life, it would have to be . . . well, actually I'm not sure. How many animals do you find tripping over their own feet? Actually, my mom's dog, Happy, once got tangled up in her tail and down she went. So I suppose I was once an animal much like Happy, oblivious to my own tail. I'd like to think in my next life I'll come back as something more refined. Maybe a swan, but probably a warthog. I suppose it takes thousands of years to fine-tune a soul like mine.

What Death Really Means

WILLOW KRAEPLIN

They say that death is frightening and horrible and scary, but I don't believe them. I have seen death, I have learned from it, and I am not afraid. I did believe them at one time. I feared death, I saw its darkness, its evil side. I saw what everyone wanted me to see. But that was before I understood. That was before I knew. I realize now that death and life are in and of each other. Death is natural and real and honest. It does a lot of things, but it never lies.

It was February, and the sky was cold and gray and frigid. It looked through us, saw our pain and glared even harder. It didn't care that we were cold. It didn't care that we had more on our minds than making sure the car was plugged in all night.

There were no clouds to speak of, just flat gray sheets that had blended into constant, hovering sky. Naked trees littered the highway we drove on, limbs drooping lifelessly, suspended above a carpet of brittle, colorless snow. The world seemed empty, and it was hard to imagine that there had ever been grass or flowers or leaves on the trees. I hated it. I cursed it.

Sometimes I would watch my mother, hands placed mechanically on the steering wheel, staring straight ahead. I tried not to bother her, partly because I knew she had enough on her mind and mostly because I knew she wasn't really there. Her body was doing what it was supposed to be doing, and we always arrived at our destination, but I usually made the trip alone.

I remember her eyes, the way they slowly lost their color and became so heavy it almost hurt to look into them. She was tired, and she had good reason to be. Her mother—my grandmother—would be dead in a few more weeks, and there was nothing we could do but watch.

My grandmother had always been a nature person. It was her influence that taught my own mother how to cherish the outdoors more than the drone of a television or the dense gaze of empty white walls. It was my grandmother's love of animals and fresh air and hardworking country life that brought me to the realization that nature was far better than any man-made structure or human creation. She knew that nature fed the imagination. She also knew that nature was hard sometimes and made you *work* hard, but it had ways of rewarding you that nothing else ever could.

She grew gardens with rows of corn and potatoes and carrots and rhubarb. She nurtured strawberries and saved them for us like rare gems, so that she could watch us pick them and eat them with as much sugar as we liked. She harvested that food, used what she could and gave away the rest.

She took nature walks and saw eagles and deer and beavers; she picked garbage from ditches and saved herself things she could collect on the shelf in her bedroom; she collected rocks—agates, mostly—and gathered cans to recycle. She walked every day, and each time nature gave her a brand new adventure. She walked until she couldn't anymore, until her body could not keep up with her determination, until the pain became enough to keep her from what she loved the most.

I think she knew before we did. She'd worked hard all her life, and she knew pain, but this was different. It was stronger. When my mother and my aunt Joann took her to the hospital, the rest of the family stayed behind to finish Thanksgiving dinner. We were worried, but we didn't expect to have only three more months with her. An ulcer maybe. Pulled muscles maybe. Cancer never.

She wanted to die at home, and we wanted her to have the option to choose such a thing, so my mother and my aunt quietly slipped into alternating roles as caretaker. My mother drove back and forth on the same stretch of blank road, coming home only for work and to sleep.

When I was able, I went with her. Each time I saw less of the grandmother I'd laughed with and loved so much, and more of the disease that was chewing her away, one day at a time.

She turned inward then; she needed distance between us, something to help her let go of what she didn't want to leave. She knew she was all alone. We could stay with her and take care of her when she could no longer take care of herself, we could give her man-made medicines to soften the pain, we could read her stories and sing her to sleep, but we could only *watch* her leave us. She was the one who had to go.

I knew that was the way it had to be—we all understood that—but it was hard to watch her leaving us behind. We weren't ready yet. We didn't want to watch such a struggle, but we loved her and we stayed. We brushed her hair and dressed her, rubbed her feet and back, sat at her bedside and read to her, fed her soup and yogurt, watched her sleep. We studied the slow, painful rise and fall of her chest, clinging to its consistency, knowing it would not last long.

Her body weakened more and more with each passing week. Before long she could no longer walk. She stopped eating. She stayed in bed and stopped talking. We gave her more of our time, which was the only thing we could give her that she could take from us. My mother took a few weeks off work to stay there with her, and my father and brother and I went as often as we could.

Spring had always been my grandmother's favorite season. It was when she grew reacquainted with the brightness of the sun, when she could go outside and sit so quietly she could almost watch the grass grow and the season shift. It was when she came alive.

With such an angry, unforgiving winter almost behind us, we hoped—for her sake—that she could hang on long enough to see the birds return and the sun flood her bedroom with the insistent force of spring. We wanted to be able to open her window and let the air rush in, sweet and heavy with the pungent aroma of new growth.

She couldn't hold on that long. So we did the next best thing. We got her a nature tape, the kind that combines the soothing caress of piano music and the kind of music that can only come from nature. As my mother and aunt and I sat near her bed, our hearts in rhythm with each shallow breath, we played the tape and the room filled with the sounds of spring. The water sang to us, soothed us, calmed us into acceptance of what we knew was coming.

My mother told her it was OK, that she could let go. We told her we would be OK. Then we watched and waited and listened, until her chest rose, then slowly drifted down and remained still. The water still flowed, the birds still sang, the piano still floated quietly around us. We cried, but we were happy. It wasn't an emotion I had not expected to feel, but it came and I welcomed it.

Her body relaxed then, and we watched the lines that had grown tight with pain slowly fade into calmness, into respite, into beauty. We took turns placing our hands over her stomach, where the cancer had taken over, a hard knot like steel between her ribs. We knew then why the fight had been one-sided from the beginning. As strong, as determined, as powerful as she was, she could have never fought such a thing.

We bathed her and washed her hair, dressed her in a favorite blue dress, kissed her good night and went upstairs to sleep. My mother and I slept together in the very same bed she'd slept in as a child, hugging one another, exhausted and relieved. We slept hard that night.

My grandmother came back that night, to visit us, to thank us for letting her die at home and to show us what we had given her. She came to Joann, light as a dream, floating up the stairs to hover there in a bright circle in the cold, dark attic air. She was young and beautiful, and her hair fanned out behind her in a wind Joann couldn't feel. She was dressed in gossamer layers of blue that billowed around her like the breath of angels. Her feet were barefoot. Her eyes shone, and her skin was so smooth and light it glowed.

She came close and leaned in to brush her lips against Joann's cheek. "Thank you for all you have done," she said and drifted away.

My family took pleasure in fulfilling my grandmother's wishes. We wrote her obituary ourselves. We built her coffin and painted it blue, then drew her favorite things all over on the outside: a log cabin, flowers, vegetables, a horse, a bluebird. She had saved the flowers from her brief hospital stay in November, had dried them and asked us to save them for this moment. So we sprinkled those inside with her, and she waited in her home while we chipped away at the frozen ground until it was ready for her. We took turns with shovels, sprinkling the earth back inside the hole, as if she were a seed we were planting. In a way she really was. She brought our family together in a way she never could have if she hadn't left us so soon.

Most people would not understand this. They want to hand over responsibility and show up at the funeral home to stand in silence above a body that has been made up and shaped to fit the way we think a dead body "should" look.

They don't want to sit with someone and watch them take their final breath without the safety of hospital lights and sounds and authority. They want to leave the hospital and return home to their own beds. They want to know that the body is spending the night in the morgue, instead of lying still and quiet just below them, in a room downstairs. They know it's OK to feel sad. What they don't know is that it's also OK to feel happy.

I used to be one of them. Because of my grandmother, I now understand that death is not such a scary thing, that it is a mere, unavoidable fact of life. I don't know why this is such a difficult thing for people to understand. In nature, death comes and goes like the change of seasons; it's a natural occurrence. Humans rely too heavily on the symbolism of death; they place too much importance on the body and on looking sad enough so that people *know* you cared. Nature simply continues to push forward.

I believe nature is a resting place for spirits. I don't feel alone when I'm in nature; it almost feels like magic sometimes, when the wind pulls tears from my eyes and whips through my hair like fingers, when the sun blinds me just enough so that I see the outline of stars when I press my eyes shut.

I think of my grandmother whenever I'm outside; I feel her with me in the warmth of the sun and in the invigorating caress of summer lake water. I smell her in the sweet, heavy air that descends on the world before a thunderstorm in spring, and I breathe in her presence when the rain has stopped and the air turns clear and strong and intoxicating.

I see her behind the glow of every rainbow, her smile spreading over my family with the strength of the sun, thanking us for giving her such a gift, thanking us for understanding what death really means.

Endings

The last essay here is one of my own. I came to it through an idea, but in the end, I abandoned the idea as my source and turned to experience. I was asked to submit an essay for an anthology about growing up in the Midwest. The anthology would be called *Townships*, and the editor hoped the essays would yield a sense of local experience, of connection to the land and people.

So I started to write. I approached my childhood neighborhood from a larger perspective, a sort of societal view, but the narrative did not hold. My comments had the ring of platitudes, and my examples seemed forced. Finally, I decided to quit thinking about the purpose of the book and to conjure instead some specific memories from my preadolescent years. I let my mind roam through memory pictures: the house, the yard, the street, the neighbors, the elementary school, my room in our house, my bed, the way the sun came in through the drawn shades in the afternoon, the tree that used to be outside that window. And then I was off, writing the story of the tree and tangential stories that came along with it the way seeds hitchhike on your clothes when you walk through the woods.

As I wrote the story, I tried to stay keen to the images that presented themselves to me, tried to be alert to meanings in them that might tell me and my reader something more about the story. The light coming through the window presages the enlightenment I was about to experience, though when I wrote that paragraph I did not know the story was about loss of innocence. I didn't realize that until my friends and siblings spilled out of the school bus at the end of the story, and I knew they did not know what I knew, and I wanted to be like the tree, wanted to hold them, like baby birds, in my hands. That is when I wrote the title: "When the Bough Breaks."

It was the best kind of writing experience: No one will be more surprised than I was by the ending.

When the Bough Breaks

SUSAN CAROL HAUSER

Townships anthology, University of Iowa Press, 1992

The early afternoon sun worked at the drawn shade of the south window. From my bed, where I was supposed to be napping, I watched. Some light sneaked in through the fabric of the shade itself. In its passage through the cream-colored fibers, it lost its edge. More yellow than

white, it breathed into the room, betraying the civiliza-
tion of dust motes that eddied about.

I almost fell asleep staring into that microcosmic
dance, but then a breeze found its way around the
outside of the house and in through my open window.
The shade was no match for it. Easily, as though with
a hand, the moving air pushed in and lifted the shade
just a little. The weight of the pine slat sewn into the
hem slapped it back down as quickly as it had risen. It
was time enough. The outside air was in, accompanied
by a stab of light. The dust motes scurried about in
panic, then quieted. Then the breeze did it again and
then again, and I wearied and slept.

I was in first grade, old enough to be conniving, but
young enough to be inept at it. I had played sick that
morning. I had to. I had asked and then begged to be
allowed to stay home from school that day. The tree
cutters were coming. They were going to saw down the
oak tree next to the house. I had tried to talk my parents out of it. They would not relent, even when I
explained about the nest, the bird nest, that I could
see from my upstairs bedroom window. The tree was
old. In the right wind, it would fall on the house. It
had to be cut down.

They said the birds would be all right. I did not
believe them. I wanted to see for myself. Would find
the nest in the fallen tree. Maybe I could hold birds
in my hands.

I thought my parents believed me when I said I was
sick. They did not argue with me. I went to my room
to wait for the men to come. Dad stayed home, too,

and also waited. When the men came, I watched him in the yard with them. Sometimes they moved around to the other side of the virgin oak, and I could not see them through the leaf-ridden branches. I could still hear their voices though, the words scrambled in their passage through space up to my window.

When it fell, the oak tree filled the entire yard. I tried to watch the branch with the nest in it plummet toward Earth, but lost it as all of the branches shuddered and collapsed into each other. I ran down the steps and out into the yard, but stopped short by the back stoop.

The tree had changed. The clusters of leaves that whispered to me in the night were gathered into fists. The branches that had held the nest out to me now kept me away from it. I tried to see it but could not. No birds flew out of the wreckage.

Then my father discovered me. I was home because I was sick. Even though I felt better, I would have to stay in my room. Already shaken by the deception of the tree, I was hit again from the other side: My father knew I had lied, and he let me get away with it.

I was glad to be going back up to my room, but when I got there, it had changed, too. With the oak tree down, the sun came straight in the south window. It illumined the grain of the knotty pine wall, and I could see how much more there was to wood than I had understood before.

I wondered what they were doing at school right now. I looked out the window in the direction of Lincoln Elementary. With the oak tree gone, I could see past the roof of Newton's garage, into Cochran's yard kitty-corner to ours and even over to the houses on the other side of Fremont Avenue, a block away. Somewhere beyond that, another dozen blocks or so, my friends and siblings were bent over their desks.

In the yard, the men were working on the tree. The smell of cut wood found its way up to me. This was familiar. There was always a new house going up in the neighborhood, and in the evening, when the carpenters were gone, we kids retook our territory. Vacant lots belonged to us and, until the grown-ups moved in, we claimed eminent domain.

We played house in those incipient homes, sawdust gripping our clothes, slivers finding the soft spots on our calloused bare feet, and the sweet odor of pine lodging forever in our hearts. Sometimes we found wood knots on the floor, and sometimes we could even find the boards they'd fallen out of. Then, sometimes, we would slip them back in, happy to see how neatly they fit and making that house somehow our own.

Sometimes, though, we kept the knots. They were red as though with the blood of the tree, and sap sometimes wept from them, and you could carry one in your pocket and reach in there for it when you needed something solid to hold onto.

In the yard, beneath my window, the men pulled the severed branches away from the tree. They dragged them over to Emerson Avenue, east of the house. The long skirts of leaves trailed behind them. I did not want to watch anymore. That was when I pulled the shade, blunting the light.

That was when I slept. When I woke, the sun had

moved on and was working its way around to the west window. Soon it would look straight in, and the other kids would be coming home from school.

I went over to that window. From there I could not see the carnage of the morning. I could see Seventy-third Street. I watched for the orange splash of the bus. For a long time the street, which did not really go anywhere, was empty. So were the yards on the other side. Like my mom, Mrs. Walters and Mrs. Kimm were in their houses. The dads were at work. Even my dad had gone back to his store.

Then the bus was there, at the corner of Fremont and Seventy-third. It stopped and the door opened, and Lottie Lee and Patty and Kippy and BeeZee and Cary Lou and Nicky and Joey and Bobbie and Diane and Kerry and Gretchen and Julie and Margaret Mary and Paul spilled out onto the road and scattered like leaves let loose in wind. Sunshine fell on them like rain. I wanted to cup my hands and gather them in.

Index